Inspiring Service

Catholic, Anglican, Methodist and Latter-day Saint Traditions in Dialogue

EDITED BY

— ANDREW TEAL —

Sacristy Press

Sacristy Press
PO Box 612, Durham, DH1 9HT

www.sacristy.co.uk

US edition first published in 2019 by the Religious Studies Center, Brigham Young University in cooperation with Deseret Book.

UK edition first published in 2020 by Sacristy Press, Durham.

Copyright © Brigham Young University 2019
The moral rights of the authors have been asserted.

All rights reserved, no part of this publication may be reproduced or transmitted in any form or by any means, electronic, mechanical photocopying, documentary, film or in any other format without prior written permission of the publisher.

Unless indicated otherwise, all images are courtesy of Simon D. Jones, copyright Intellectual Reserve, Inc.

Scripture quotations, unless otherwise stated, are from the New Revised Standard Version Bible: Anglicized Edition, copyright © 1989, 1995 National Council of the Churches of Christ in the United States of America. Used by permission. All rights reserved worldwide.

Every reasonable effort has been made to trace the copyright holders of material reproduced in this book, but if any have been inadvertently overlooked the publisher would be glad to hear from them.

Sacristy Limited, registered in England & Wales, number 7565667

British Library Cataloguing-in-Publication Data
A catalogue record for the book is available from the British Library

ISBN 978-1-78959-129-3

With profound affection, this volume is dedicated to

Elder Jeffrey R. Holland and Sister Patricia Holland of
the Church of Jesus Christ of Latter-day Saints, whose
visit to Oxford prompted this genuine dialogue

and to other contributors and their respective traditions—

The Rt Hon. The Lord Alton of Liverpool
The Most Revd & Rt Hon. The Lord Williams of Oystermouth
The Revd Professor Frances Young

—*in anticipation of further committed and fruitful collaboration.*

Contents

Acknowledgements v
Contributors vii

Introduction *Andrew Teal* 1

1. **Inspiring Service** *Andrew Teal with David Alton, Jeffrey R. Holland, Rowan Williams, Frances Young* 19
2. **The Restored Gospel** *Jeffrey R. Holland with Andrew Teal* 71
3. **Christmas Comfort** *Jeffrey R. Holland* 97

Index 102

Acknowledgements

We acknowledge with gratitude the cooperation and generosity of many in enabling the visit of Elder Jeffrey R. Holland and Sister Patricia Holland to Oxford in November 2018.

The Church of Jesus Christ of Latter-day Saints has been consistently generous in its kindness, flexibility, and significant, continued support of the project.

Thanks are due to Oxford University's Faculty of Theology and Religion and to Professors Keith Ward, Carol Harrison, and Joel Rasmussen—among many others—for support and participation in this project.

In addition to the speakers who contributed to the panel discussion, we are grateful to the University Church of St. Mary the Virgin and its vicar, the Reverend Dr William Lamb, for hosting the presentation by Elder Holland and the response by Andrew Teal. Additionally, we thank Paul Kerry for chairing that event.

Thanks also go to Pembroke College Oxford, which hosted the large audience at the presentations; to the Rev. W. N. Monteith Charitable Trust for their donation; and to the porters, events staff, chefs, and hall staff of Pembroke College, who are all thanked sincerely for their hospitality and considerable hard work.

The choir, organist, and choir director of the Damon Wells Chapel are thanked for their welcome and contribution in presenting "Nine Lessons and Carols" as the context for Elder Holland's "Christmas Comfort" address.

Special thanks are due to Professor Richard Williams of the BYU Wheatley Institution for the artwork and publicity, to Professor David Kirkham of BYU London Centre for transport provision, to the Programme for the Foundation of Law and Constitutional Government at the University of Oxford Law Faculty, to BYU International Centre for Law and Religious Studies, and to Professor Brett Scharffs's support of the panel banquet. The transformation of a series of public events into a book has been possible only by the skilful industry of the BYU Religious Education Faculty Support Center, student employees who created typescripts, and the Religious Studies Center staff who edited, designed, and published the book, among them especially Scott C. Esplin, R. Devan Jensen, Brent R. Nordgren, Emily Cook, Abigail Crimm, and Emily V. Strong; thanks also to Rachel Teal and Chris Long for their skills and suggestions.

Most significantly, thanks are due to Paul Kerry for his continued support, expertise, and meticulous attention to detail in arranging, checking, and enabling the event and publication. It is acknowledged with profound admiration and respect and sincere thanks for his love, service, and capability, without which neither the "Inspiring Service" events nor this book would have come to fruition.

May this work testify to the generosity and faithfulness of God, contribute to the reconciliation of Christian communities represented herein, and mark a significant step in the development of beautiful friendships and respectful theological explorations.

Andrew Teal

Contributors

David, Lord Alton, a senior lay British Catholic, is very active in the political life of the nation and the world. He is a former Liberal Party and later Liberal Democrat Member of Parliament who has sat as a cross-bench member of the House of Lords since 1997. He is known for his human rights work, including the co-founding of Jubilee Action, the children's charity now known as Chance for Childhood. He is also Professor of Citizenship at Liverpool John Moores University.

Elder Jeffrey R. Holland was ordained a member of the Quorum of the Twelve Apostles of The Church of Jesus Christ of Latter-day Saints in 1994. He was the ninth president of Brigham Young University. He was president of the American Association of Presidents of Independent Colleges and Universities and is known for his work with understanding communities that are being persecuted, especially conflict between Christians and Jews (he was given a Torch of Liberty for that work), and supporting the plight of dispossessed and refugee communities such as the Yazidis.

The Reverend Dr Andrew Teal has been a full member of Oxford's Faculty of Theology and Religion since 2008. He has been an admissions coordinator, disability officer, harassment advisor, and teacher of New Testament Greek across the university and a Pro-Proctor of the university for two seasons. He is chaplain, fellow, and lecturer in theology at Pembroke College Oxford, teaching historical and systematic theology; the history of Christianity; and the study of religions, with research interests especially in patristic and modern theology, Christology and ecclesiology, Eastern Orthodox theology and interfaith dialogue, theology and the arts, and theology and frontier spirituality. He is especially committed to furthering theological understanding in dialogue with The Church of Jesus Christ of Latter-day Saints.

Rowan, Lord Williams is a Welsh Anglican bishop, theologian, and poet. He was also the 104th Archbishop of Canterbury, Metropolitan and Primate of all England, and leader as First Among Equals of the Anglican community worldwide from 2003 until 2012. Previously, he was Bishop of Monmouth, Archbishop of Wales, and Regius Professor of Divinity and Canon of Christ Church at Oxford. He is now Master of Magdalen College in Cambridge.

The Reverend Professor Frances Young taught theology at the University of Birmingham from 1971 to 2002. While there, she was an Edward Cadbury Professor, head of the Department of Theology, Dean of the Faculty of Arts, and Pro-Vice-Chancellor. She is also an ordained Methodist minister, which allows her to serve and preach in a deprived, formerly industrial Methodist circuit of the West Midlands, while continuing to pursue academic service. She writes about Christianity in its formative centuries, as well as the New Testament. Additionally, she has reflected publicly, at personal cost, upon her experience of being the mother of Arthur, her firstborn son, who was born with profound disabilities. She has worked in the theological and ecumenical dimensions with L'Arche communities and the Faith and Light movement together with Canadian Catholic philosopher, theologian, and humanitarian Jean Vanier.

Introduction

Andrew Teal

The genesis of an idea

I begin with a disclaimer. It is all the more interesting, moving, and challenging to dive straight into this volume's records of an extraordinary weekend in Oxford towards the end of Michaelmas term in 2018 than to begin bogged down in this introductory description, commentary, and agenda. I am persuaded to submit an introduction only on the understanding that readers are forewarned that it is a retrospective reflection that aims to give some context to the event, to offer some reflective commentary on the sessions, and most of all to invite us to look forward, presenting some outcomes. In that sense, better an introduction than a conclusion.

The notion of a panel of speakers from across Christian traditions emerged through friendship. Matthew Holland, then the president of Utah Valley University, spent a term as a visiting scholar at Pembroke College Oxford; he was very good news and someone adept at initiating fruitful conversations across the University of Oxford and further afield. As a result, I was delighted to be part of a meeting of faith leaders exploring the plight of the Yazidis, where Elder Jeffrey R. Holland and Sister Patricia Holland joined Baroness Nicholson, Bishop Alastair Redfern, Lord Alton, and many others to be in solidarity with religious freedom in general and the Yazidis community in particular.

In conversations there, especially with Paul Kerry, two other concerns emerged:

1. How might we find ways of inspiring students and young people to take to heart a sense of vocation rather than merely an oppressive

awareness of the large amount of student debt to be managed after they graduate? In other words, how could we unleash and energize a sense of vocation?

2. There was some reflection about the place of worship and college chaplaincy in higher education, in particular how—in the college chapels of Oxford and Cambridge—beautiful, aesthetic experiences are so often limited to fleeting emotions without encouraging a profound engagement with the substance of faith and its capacity to reach deeply into, and transform, the human condition. It was agreed that as marvellous as it was that literary and musical accomplishments celebrated human creativity and beauty, enabling the possibility of meaningful pastoral connections, the spontaneous desire to share the greatest gift, that of faith in a loving God worthy of the outpouring of such worship, was hard to convey and sometimes even avoided and treated as an embarrassment.

Inspiring service

There thus seemed to be an important agenda, a real opportunity to begin to address these needs together, so bringing together a spectrum of people that were able to do something about it would be the best strategy. It was never going to be handed to us on a plate, we needed a significant amount of energy and a year and a half to imagine, plan, and provide for such an opportunity that might address these perceived needs. Paul Kerry's organizational commitment and contagious enthusiasm never waned; the idea of a panel of speakers from the Church, academy, and public and political service was conceived.

This had the obvious advantage of addressing issues by looking to serve the world, looking outward together from a spectrum of faith perspectives in a mission that sought to communicate the value of all and to equip people to respond to needs boldly, collaboratively using diverse gifts, talents, energy, and personalities to transform our world. This notion was simple and clear. The academy is a proper environment to equip leaders to a model of profound service: leadership in Church, state, and local communities needs an integrity that measures power in the currency of service and values. The emergent idea of "Inspiring Service" sought to prompt people to reflect upon their experiences to equip a new generation to make a difference—contributing at a formative time in the life of students to use and cherish established, trusting relationships.

Thankfully this brought together four outstanding public servants—in state, academy, and Church—to commit to come to Oxford to meet students and others, formally at a panel and then informally over a stunningly large and inclusive banquet dinner, enabled by generous donations.

David Alton

Lord Alton began the series of presentations with an address that was as personal as it was carefully structured. He explored principles that must guide and inspire in the political world; he reflected upon appropriate, reflective, and informed practice, before acknowledging in a poignant manner how it is personhood that inspires most powerfully. In a world where contemporary political life seems dominated by the charisma of personality, and where there is significant evidence of popularist propaganda, Lord Alton urged a virtue ethic with these three dimensions—where values, honest reflection, and paradigms of personhood as character stand firmly against quick-fix techniques of an ethic rooted in personality or charisma.

Lord Alton cited examples from across his political career. As the youngest-ever Liberal Councillor (aged twenty-one), he took a seat on Liverpool City Council in 1971. He was elected Member of Parliament as a member of the Liberal Party (later the Liberal Democrats) from 1979–97, and is currently a cross-bench peer in the House of Lords. He managed to balance his integrity with the machinations of politics, but would not compromise his commitment to human rights at every stage of human life—particularly aligning himself with the vulnerable. He is Professor of Citizenship at John Moores University in Liverpool and is committed to human rights, religious freedoms, and inspiring the International Young Leaders Network. His address and answers to the questions show that this is not a mere strategic or superficial veneer but his very life as a committed Catholic rooted in the social teaching of his own faith community. Alluding to Gandhi, Lord Alton himself demonstrated that integrity consists of ourselves being the change we want to see in our world and brought the personal plights of victims of religious oppression into the discussion with vigour and commitment.

Jeffrey R. Holland
Elder Holland brought his pastoral genius and his experience as president of Brigham Young University and a member of the Quorum of the Twelve Apostles in The Church of Jesus Christ of Latter-day Saints, where he has had significant international leadership experience. He established that the character of the giver is laid bare in acts of service informed by committed understanding. Elder Holland's address focused on the stories of the New Testament, particularly the story of the Good Samaritan (Luke 10:30–37), to show the centrality of service within the Christian faith tradition—service extended to all regardless of differences in belief. Anything that gets in the way of caring for another, whether it is dressed up as business or a desire to not be made ritually unclean by an encounter, is exposed as a reluctance to be "doers of the word" (James 1:22), and disobedience to the requirements to give energy and attention empathetically to anyone; "if a brother or sister is naked and lacks daily food" (James 2:15), then words are not an adequate response to authentic philanthropy. He encouraged quiet and sustainable service rather than self-promotion and cited the Book of Mormon (Alma 34:17–28) as a witness and guide consistent with the teachings of the New Testament.

Elder Holland is a member of the Quorum of the Twelve Apostles of The Church of Jesus Christ of Latter-day Saints, a church renowned for generously modelling the centrality of worship and community service; the imperative of giving sacrificially for humanitarian, welfare, and educational impact; a profound commitment to interfaith collaboration, advocacy, and solidarity, speaking for human rights and religious freedom; and support for international governance with finance and friendship. He acknowledged the traumatic experience of being a persecuted minority in that Church's early days—in the state of Missouri and in the Roman Empire centuries ago—as significant motivation for this outward-looking service. Yet his own community's accomplishments were not Elder Holland's emphasis. Rather, he focused on the witness of scripture and the potential each person has (giving Saint Teresa of Calcutta as an example) to change the world and its future, offering an antidote to widespread cynicism concerning the motivations and impact of serving and the unselfish use of human agency. The references to the New Testament illuminate a much-cited text from the Book of Mormon: 2 Nephi 25:23. This text is often cited by the Reformed tradition as evidence that the restored Church is one of works-righteousness. Rather, this text urges profound accountability and may also be read as a text that heralds the victory of grace; despite the immensely inspiring examples of so many, salvation is rooted in God's saving will and power. But the text may be read as highlighting this further, taking the phrase "that it is by grace that we are saved, after all we can do" as an affirmation of the power of God to bring victory and light out of all the dark deeds that humanity can—and does—do,[1] as well as exhorting our efforts to bear all the fruits of "love, joy, peace, patience, kindness, generosity, faithfulness, gentleness and self-control" (Galatians 5:22–23).

There is a rare mixture of energetic encouragement and realism in this contribution, illustrative of the particular contribution of this faith tradition to an informed and intelligent mission to the world—holding together a conviction in the action and sovereignty of God, with the imperative of moral volition and agency in all our faculties and energies.

Rowan Williams

Lord Williams's experience in the academy, Church, British state, and world affairs is almost unique. Having been Regius Professor of Divinity in the University of Oxford (1986–91), he was consecrated to serve as bishop of Monmouth, thereafter archbishop of the Church in Wales (2000–2), and, between 2002 and 2012, he was Archbishop of Canterbury, Primate of all England, and First Among Equals of the worldwide Anglican Communion of eighty-seven million people. After retiring from that role, he was appointed Master of Magdalene College Cambridge and life peer—as Baron Williams of Oystermouth—in 2013. Lord Williams has thus not only managed to hold together very significant roles in different arenas but also reconciled his own clear convictions with an awareness that leadership was not about what he *felt* about a matter. Thus equipped, he managed, almost against all odds, to hold together very divergent theologies within the Anglican Communion.

In his contribution, cooperation is core to his understanding of fulfilment and altruism in close relation: "The self-interest of wanting to be myself most fully is, paradoxically, interest in learning how I'm most free to serve and to nourish my neighbour." Personal competition does not contribute to the accomplishment of the whole, and individualism even in team endeavours threatens the accomplishment of the best outcome through cooperative virtue. Lord Williams argues that this level of aspiration builds upon the three Ps of Lord Alton—principles, practice, and people—with the notion of prophecy, challenging idolatry and unfaithfulness. Prophecy can be challenging for us because it is often catastrophized or conceived of melodramatically. Lord Williams refers to the imperative, if uncomfortable, prophetic tradition of challenging the myths we live by. Such realistic prophecy is rooted in a fifth P—prose. In a world that prefers the poetic and creative and so easily undervalues the prosaic, hard, and routine, detailed work is imperative. It establishes the system to check another P—permission. In particular, part of pushing out into the deep and attempting responsible agency amid enormous and seemingly insoluble difficulties has to be risky. There has to be the permission not to be perfect, not to be God, the permission to fail as we address personal wounds and structural problems of our life in this world. The kind of human being we wish to be is intimately tangled up with the sort of opportunities we create for other human beings to flourish.

Frances Young
Professor Young's presentation has characteristics of a Methodist testimony. But as she has been aware of the tendency of testimonies to bear witness to oneself, her presentation is executed in a sophisticated style. She owns the demands of the example of her father, Stanley Worrell, who also translated some very significant texts concerned with understanding early Christianity. For all that, Professor Young's most significant self-designation is that of a "presbyter of the universal Church and one of John Wesley's preachers"; in other words, holding together ministerial sacrifice and pedagogy. That priesthood is articulated as the

leitmotif of service and echoes the awareness of the Eastern tradition, which she understands so well and which intuitively shapes her service: "Priesthood, for me," wrote Alexander Elchaninov, "means the possibility of speaking with a full voice".[2]

Much of her life consists of holding apparently different things together creatively; the critic and the visionary, the scholar and the pastor, the mother and a leader of the academy, and speaking and acting convincingly and with balance—with a full voice. With this voice, her writings and preaching seek to reach out to those different from herself with an eye for connection. In a world where individuation and individualism are the measure of success, Professor Young urges a valuing of institutions as a means of requiring corporateness and cooperation and recovering community. Emergence does not only refer to the enhanced capacities of slime mould under certain situations but also to what human beings are for: to grow into the stature of Christ together. In this way, we can transform the disenchantments and disillusionments that we encounter, such as the response Professor Young received from an elder statesman of Methodism when she asked about what place there was in Methodism for a woman theologian. His reply—"None"—simply urged her on, as did the disincentivizing feedback from her classics professor at the end of her preliminary year as an undergraduate. She took C. K. Barrett's commentary on the Greek text of the Gospel of John and "picked up and read". For all its vividness, Professor Young's encouragement is far from sentimental or emotive.

Eating together

One of the most moving and authentic aspects of the evening, after drinks and conversations outside the lecture theatre, was the banquet dinner in Pembroke Hall for 150 people.

Inevitably, Orthodox metropolitans, archbishops, professors, heads of Oxford colleges, bishops, archpriests, and the great and the good from university, Church, and city were present. Also present were people who had been invited because they lived in hostels or had spent many years living on the street, recovering from self-medications of various sorts—drugs, alcohol, and so forth—who were welcomed with generous, authentic affection, which recognized the dignity of all present. There were also local church members and undergraduate and graduate students in attendance.

In a nutshell, it was a foretaste of the heavenly banquet and modelled what the professor of government and politics Stephen Whitefield styled "commensality": being together around one table, being nourished together, sharing friendship, and modelling dignity together. This was a most moving and delightful celebration, which is not referred to here as there were no further formal contributions. The Master of Pembroke College welcomed all present and gratefully recalled her own ecumenical background—one steeped in Quaker and Methodist Church practice and Anglicanism at school—which, she appreciated, had steered her to nurture a sense of responsibility and service.

The inclusion of people with acknowledged addictions prompted a sensitivity and analytical self-awareness among many participants. One person reflected upon why he and so many people so often choose to live and die with addictions: because the dawning awareness of the pain of taking responsibility for actions and habits can simply feel too hard, too much to acknowledge and face, and the comfortably numb experience of an anaesthetized existence is easier.

Eating together is rarely an occasion for such introspection, even the retelling of this story (with permission) makes the event sound rather intense. The fact was that eating together, even in the formal context of an Oxford college hall, was an opportunity for growth in honesty, personal integrity, and trust. The truth, as it were, made itself known in the breaking of bread.

Theological Investigations Concerning the Restored Gospel of Jesus Christ

Although the idea of a panel was conceived first, a persistent thought pursued us: whilst it is a duty and a joy to focus outwards in generosity, what about those things that are of first-order theological concern? What of those differences that have divided the Christian family across the ages, and in particular since the visions of the young Joseph Smith Jr. and the establishment of the restored Church of Jesus Christ of Latter-day Saints? Was a theological exploration and dialogue too much to hope for? A panel would allow common purpose, as can be seen from the papers delivered and the questions asked. Would a theological discussion highlight differences in approach? Indeed, was a theological investigation not bound to illustrate a fundamental difficulty in a community still open to the voice of living prophecy in its leadership and Church authority and therefore perhaps more cautious of theological enterprises? The assumption that theologians are somehow spiritual authorities as well as scholarly specialists has resulted in examples of assertiveness and disorder, which has led to division and a lack of cohesion in the history of the Church.

Thankfully, the Faculty of Theology and Religion put its name to such an initial investigation, and the University Church of St. Mary the Virgin hosted an engagement despite concerns on their behalf that this might be stepping back from scholarly or Anglican models of dissipated authority and freedom of scholarship. The presentation and discussion took place in a historically significant venue for theological discussion, indeed where Thomas Cranmer had been condemned and led to his execution outside in Broad Street in March 1556. Elder Jeffrey R. Holland, however, was sincerely and warmly welcomed as he made a humble and generous-minded address leading into a theological exploration of the restored gospel. This was, in fact, the first of the three events recorded here: on Thursday, 22 November, Oxford added another name to its historical Apostles and witnesses. From the first moment that Elder and Sister Holland arrived on the High Street, with Jacob, their guide from Salt Lake City, a sense of restored perspective and true affection and friendship was palpable and self-evident. This was not going to be a dry argument over minutiae of detail and disagreement, but a recovery of life and joy in a spirit of joyful appreciation and open dialogue. Whilst this was not the initial primary purpose of a visit, it became a core and commanding event, which required minds and hearts and a willingness to listen, while being as true as possible to our experiences. Truthfulness of conversation strove to be the most inclusive dialogue—where truth, fairness, and kindness moved to the most fruitful hopes, open in scope.

Elder Holland began his address to the academy at Oxford with some basic clarifications, which addressed some popular misconceptions and misrepresentations. He unapologetically outlined the beliefs of his community, including the vision of Joseph Smith Jr. in 1820, where Father and Son appeared in a glory that exceeded "the brightness of the sun" (Joseph Smith—History 1:16), but that vision, for all its wonder, was but a precursor of all that would unfold, including a visit to the oldest university in Britain to engage in a series of conversations with openness and hope.

Elder Holland explored the confusion and conflict that so often characterized the Latter-day Saint experience. It was a community thrust into the experience of having an extermination order issued against them, which enflamed a persecuting mob.

What comes across is that these outcasts, though fleeing to the West amid great trauma, did not seek to withdraw from the world but took steps to become a US state and got involved in the social, political, and, of course, religious life of the young nation. That energetic commitment is evident in the fact that members of the Latter-day Saint community remain so publicly involved and, indeed, are in many ways the epitome of the American dream, finding faith and trust that—despite all initial appearances—there is something ultimately providential about the American Constitution. However, as The Church of Jesus Christ of Latter-day Saints becomes more international, questions about accommodations of American culture to indigenous lifestyles have made the addressing issues of enculturation an important task.

Elder Holland, acutely aware of the trauma that the Christian churches have inflicted and suffered, was rightly cautious in his response to my question about recognition of the dignity and purposes of Joseph Smith Jr. among other Christian traditions. He would hope for that, but he had a firm grasp of reality. After all, the historic divisions since the Council of Chalcedon (AD 451), the Great Schism between Eastern and Western Christians (before AD 1054), and the Protestant Reformation and Catholic Counter-Reformations (ca. 1517 onwards) remain festering wounds in Christendom. Even recent attempts at rapprochement between Anglican and Methodist ministry and recognition in the UK have still failed.[3] Commitment to theological exploration and consultation would have to be miraculous to achieve where centuries of attempted reconciliation have failed.

Perhaps that has something to do with an over-assertive "can-do"—or, better, a Babel—attitude rather than a humble one that brings everything together with an openness for this to be the work of God, rather than the reforming good ideas of human beings. Such a commitment is less another attempt at reformation than an openness to restoration. That happens only with our asking God to guide and sustain us. Timing—as in comedy and cooking—is everything, and the achievement depends on God's timing rather than our pushing.

Dare we hope with Elder Holland? Could it possibly be that these problematic days for the mainstream churches be the very time when God may act? As Eastern Christians gather for the Orthodox Liturgy, a deacon says to the presiding priest, "Now it is time for the Lord to act" (cf. Psalm 119:126); it is not our action, though it requires of us both volition and a willingness not to get in the way. "Inspiring Service" and the events around it hold out before us the imperative of a near-impossible task. John Donne brings us close to an inclusive vision that can only be the work of the infinite atoning power of Jesus Christ:

> For all this separation, Christ Jesus is amongst us all, and in His time, will break downe the wall too, these differences amongst Christians, and make us glad of that name, the name of Christians, without affecting ourselves, or inflicting upon others, the names of envy, and subdivision.[4]

Outcomes

The outcomes from this encounter certainly remain fruitful and promise a harvest still to be reaped. Elder Holland was more than good with his word of inviting me to Utah, and a first visit to Salt Lake City followed. It focused on Temple Square, the general conference of spring 2019, the work and inspiring service of Welfare Square, and the academic work of Brigham Young University—in particular its Religious Studies Center and the Neal A. Maxwell Institute for Religious Scholarship.

As wonderful as these outcomes were for me personally, there was—and remains—a sense that these opportunities are far too significant (and far too enormous!) to be mine alone. Further visits have been planned, participation in conferences considering the nature of chaplaincy from various faith perspectives have been discussed, and proposed scholarly enterprises in Provo, Oxford, and even mainland Europe that engage in scholarship from a wide spectrum of traditions are to be worked at.

Although it is a personal privilege to form relationships in the service of God and address the world's needs, it is too small a thing considering the responsibilities we bear for our own faith communities: to encourage peoples to "travel" together is imperative and foundational work. To enable this work is a burning priority, whether we see an outcome in our days on earth or not.

Integrity is imperative; every one of us has a personal responsibility to engage with an eye to being an ambassador for Christ and the community of which we are a part. That clarity of purpose cannot seek to feign, but to engender friendships, encouraging faith and service from the perspective of becoming a committed auxiliary, not of pretending to be a member of each other's church.[5]

In my conversation with Elder Holland during the question-and-answer session, I referred to the disappointing ruling in Leo XIII's apostolic letter *Apostolicae Curae* (1896) for Anglo-Catholics. It judged Anglican orders to be "absolutely null and utterly void". In fact, it merely said that an Anglican priest is not a (Roman) Catholic priest. The Anglican Church really does not hold a coherent view of priesthood across the spectrum of its own groupings, but for all the pain of its clarity, Leo XIII's letter does not deny Anglican ministry and service. Real discussion faces uncomfortable histories and difficult categories; to commit ourselves to this theological journey will mean travelling a steep and narrow path and bearing the pain so that it, and we, might be transformed.

Thus, whilst we may dare to harbour hopes of unity and respect—such as the representation of The Church of Jesus Christ of Latter-day Saints on the World Council of Churches as observers—of an embrace of *sobornost* (ecumenicity), or the universal recognition of baptism and appreciation of diversity—those worthy aspirations are not why we must be committed to deeper understanding. Elder Holland insisted upon anchoring our energies upon something at once more straightforward and demanding: "The first obligation forever and ever, is that we love God and love each other. If we could remember that, begin with that, and do that, I can't really imagine a serious conversation getting into trouble."

Worship: "Nine Lessons and Carols"

The conclusion of weekly services in the Damon Wells Chapel in Pembroke College Oxford on the last Sunday of Michaelmas term is the traditional "Nine Lessons and Carols" service, originating in King's College, Cambridge, but applied to Pembroke's royal and religious foundation. Readings from the Old and New Testaments point to the person of Jesus Christ and the significance of His birth. At the conclusion of their visit to Oxford, Elder and Sister Holland attended this service before a formal "High Table" in Pembroke Hall.

The chapel, seating a maximum of 110 people, contained 156 people that night. The choir sang a mixture of anthems, and the congregation joined in with carols. Nine readers from the college read the lessons, and, at the end, Elder Holland gave a poignant but simple address, which is printed in its entirety in this book.

Had people expected a cheerful, plastic, prepacked, nonchalant address, they would have been profoundly disappointed. The *words* are printed in this book, but it was the humble, engaging *manner* in which they were delivered that grasped the attention of people's minds and hearts.

One guest was a retired Fellow whose wife of very many years had recently died. He telephoned me afterwards to say that he hadn't quite known what to expect, but the way Elder Holland drew on personal pain at this season could not have been more appropriate for him: it brought him comfort (the etymological root of that is strengthening). There was neither a forced smile in sight nor an expectation to be cheerful. Rather, there was an embracing humanity and solidarity at a time of loss and pain.

A member of the choir who describes herself as a "post-Christian feminist" remarked that although she did not share his faith, she saw in

Elder Holland a pastor par excellence—a very humane and endearing man, who drew close to people with authenticity. Elder Holland's address is inclusive and encouraging without abandoning the invitation that goes with proclaiming the Good News; it fitted the subdued and gently lit environment of a college chapel. Elder Holland appeared as someone as prone to human joys and pains and weakness as anyone else, and because of this, he drew close enough to be trusted. He did this while witnessing that he had been led into life and was therefore worth following. Elder Holland has the gift of using beautifully crafted prose, but he offered a means of preaching the gospel without the din of words. He humbly walked the path that the families of Christian communities must walk, together, with gentle faith, joyful hope, and authentic love.

Conclusions—Ambassadors of Love

In the panel presentations we see that testimony given from one life to another is most moving and compelling. Such communication faces disenchantment—even a negative response to Frances Young's question about women theologians became a challenging and creative "no" to her, as did her wait for ordination within her tradition until the time was right.

It is easy to be impatient and to wish to travel by ourselves to an ideal destination. Dietrich Bonhoeffer is right to remind us that when we put our personal ideas above given values held by a community, we become a despiser of the community of which we are a part because it cannot keep up or measure up to our idea of perfection:

> It means, first, that a Christian needs others because of Jesus Christ. It means, second, that a Christian comes to others only through Jesus Christ. It means, third, that in Jesus Christ we have been chosen from eternity, accepted in time, and united for eternity. He who loves his dream of a community more than the Christian community itself becomes a destroyer of the latter, even though his personal intentions may be ever so honest and earnest and sacrificial.[6]

It is also easy to imagine naively that good relationships and theological engagement and listening are not already happening. There are wonderful examples of good relationships between the churches. Yet there is something especially significant about the events in Oxford, which brought together the Oxford academy with that of Utah and put in one line representatives of Roman Catholic, Anglican, Restorationist, and Methodist Christian traditions. Together, they looked at questions and needs of the world. There are different models of authority, from the Catholic hierarchy, to the dissipated model of Anglican and Methodist authority, to a church that has living prophets, seers, and revelators—of which Elder Holland is one.

There are therefore significant questions worthy of exploration that became clear, but these emerged in an environment of profound friendship and love—embodying a sense of God's mission to the world, rather than competing denominations diminishing each other.

It is in this mode of dialogue, in real Christian love, that there is a fundamentally hopeful invitation to explore things that on the surface would appear to be areas of contradiction and conflict, but which—as illustrated by Professor Young—are a possibility for extraordinary service and achievement as one connected web.

With the experience of these series of events still alive in Oxford, it is very easy to be over-optimistic, and we know that with that comes disillusionment and despair. Elder Holland's response to the question about a wider appreciation of Joseph Smith Jr. was helpful here: he would long for that, but he is not unrealistic about the struggle, the steep trail of faith, that lies ahead on that route. The Christian Church cannot reform itself; a restoration which is nothing other than the work of God is required. If it is of God, it is also too important to rush. Impatience often rejects the commitment to make changes slowly for the good of all. The events in Oxford leave questions and intuitions.

The work of theological and spiritual engagement with one another in God's mission to the world is too important just to be a marginal or eccentric scholarly interest. This engagement has to be on behalf of and offered to our communities. The experience has stirred in me a desire to dedicate scholarship, devotion, and myself to the path of reconciliation—for the glory of God, the good of the Church, and the needs of the world that God loves. But it cannot merely be a personal journey; it is a long and no doubt problematic path to be travelled with our communities.

Anything less is too cautious and too unadventurous. Might it even be that Joseph Smith Jr.'s experience is a shocking surprise to the Christian Church still? That asking how to proceed and being met by the purposeful, redemptive presence of the Heavenly Father through the life and ministry of his Son and through the Holy Ghost sharing that divine nature might restore the divine dignity of the children of God in our flesh and in our day? Might what has been so misconstrued and misunderstood as diminution yet be the liberating truth that the God of earth and heaven desires to draw close to each person and that the talents and energies we have need to address this?

The events of "Inspiring Service," through the many contributions, invite us to travel beyond brittle conceptions of our self into the whole history of humanity, with the mission of redeeming by friendship and service. That can only ever be accomplished as an act of love.

> *In heaven, where we shall know God,*
>   *there may be no use of faith;*
> *In heaven, where we shall see God, there may be no use of hope;*
> *But in heaven, where God the Father, and the Son,*
>   *love one another in the Holy Ghost, the bond of*
>   *charity shall everlastingly unite us together.*[7]

Notes

1. Some read "after all that we can do" in a negative sense—as in after all that human beings are capable of doing, and have done through history, God's grace will accomplish salvation. However, it is clear that the positive encouragement of this verse has priority—urging us to do all that we can but remain humble even in that enthusiasm, to see the work of God as sovereign.
2. Alexander Elchaninov, *The Diary of a Russian Priest* (London: Faber & Faber, 1973), p. 18.
3. The Anglican Methodist reunion scheme failed in 1972 and has consistently failed to be approved, even in the General Synod of the Church of England in the summer of 2019. "General Synod: Methodist Union Legislation a Bridge too Far for Now", *Church Times*, 12 July 2019.
4. John Donne, Sermons II.3.615–19, in *One Equall Light: An Anthology of the Writings of John Donne*, comp. and ed. John Moses (Norwich: Canterbury Press, 2003), p. 35.
5. Compare Robert L. Millet, "God Grants unto All Nations", in the 2019 conference of the Society of Mormon Philosophers and Theologians, University of Utah, 15 March 2019, pp. 4–5 (typescript): "It does not mean that God disapproves of or rejects all that devoted seekers after truth are teaching or doing, where their heart is, and what they hope to accomplish in the religious world. 'God, the Father of us all,' President Ezra Taft Benson said, 'uses the men of the earth, especially good men, to accomplish his purposes. It has been true in the past, it is true today, it will be true in the future.' President Benson then quoted the following from a conference address delivered by Elder Orson F. Whitney in 1928: 'Perhaps the Lord needs such men on the outside of His Church to help it along. They are among its auxiliaries, and can do more good for the cause where the Lord has placed them, than anywhere else.' Now, note this particularly poignant message: 'God is using more than one people for the accomplishment of His great and marvellous work. The Latter-day Saints cannot do it all. It is too vast, too arduous for any one people.'"
6. Dietrich Bonhoeffer, *Life Together*, trans. John W. Doberstein (London: SCM Press, 1985), pp. 10–11, 15–16.
7. John Donne, Sermons II.10.15–19, in Moses, *One Equall Light*, p. 44.

1

Inspiring Service

*Andrew Teal with David Alton, Jeffrey R. Holland,
Rowan Williams and Frances Young*

The following remarks were presented at the "Inspiring Service" panel at Pembroke College, University of Oxford, 23 November 2018.

Andrew Teal

Welcome to Pembroke College for this important event.[1] I'm going to stand a bit away from the conventional opening of a conference. I'm going to share a small introduction for each of our guests, but you already know these people, I hope. So at the outset I testify what a great privilege it is to be here; I am not feigning it when I say what a tremendous privilege it is to welcome you all to an important event in the life of Pembroke, indeed in my life, and hopefully in the lives of faith and wider communities in our world as we listen to people who want to encourage us to be who we really are and grow together into what we might become. I utterly respect our speakers in very different ways. I have, without any caveat, a massive respect for people who have given up their time to come to us, to pass along their own experience, and to give energy and direction to us in our lives. Thank you so much for coming; it really means a great deal.

In addition to our speakers tonight, we welcome guests who represent world faiths: Metropolitan Kallistos (Ware) of Diokleia of the Greek Orthodox community; Archpriest Stephen Platt of the Russian Orthodox community in Oxford; and Bishop Humphrey Southern, representing the Diocese of Oxford. International aid agencies are represented—the international director of CAFOD (the Catholic Fund for Overseas Development), Geoff O'Donoghue, is here among them—as are religious communities of different denominations, some of whom are literally very visible: the Anglican Carmelite Sisters of the Love of God and their Reverend Mother, Sister Clare-Louise SLG, and the Society of Jesus, whose Head of Formation, Father Nicholas King, is hiding here at the front. It is excellent to have you all here. Welcome, too, to those from the academy and diverse representatives of political, public, and religious life—all supportive of this conference's attempt to serve people in their quest to find what they are for.

Some people who are not here this evening have asked me to pass on their greetings. His Eminence Cardinal Vincent Nichols, archbishop of Westminster and the head of the 4.2 million Catholics of England and Wales, has asked me to share this with you:

> I willingly offer my prayers and blessing for the initiative "Inspiring Service", taking place in Pembroke College. The note of service is crucially important to the health of our society because there is in all genuinely human transactions an element of gratuity as explored by Pope Benedict XVI in his encyclical *Caritas in Veritate*. I hope your reflections and conversation together offer inspiration and a vision of hope and unity for all those who wish to make the characteristic of service a key element in their vocation choice.

The Anglican Church has about eighty-five million members worldwide, and the Right Reverend Alastair Redfern, formerly Bishop of Derby, and now Bishop Advisor on interfaith issues to the Archbishop of Canterbury at Lambeth Palace, also greets us:

> I am delighted to offer support for this significant gathering at Pembroke College. From national initiatives to Diocesan and parish projects, the Anglican Church seeks to fulfil a vocation to serve the neediest in our own society and across the globe—often in partnership with those of other Christian traditions and with those of other Faiths.
>
> The common driver in seeking to acknowledge the preciousness of God's image in all people, and especially in those who are in particular need, is the desire to share together in the creation of confidence, hope, and the experiencing of shared goodness and grace.
>
> Your conference will enable participants to explore their own contribution, and that of their networks, to this vital work of creating community and a connected citizenship—inspiring service to enable reconciliation and encourage hope in the future. The measure of the health of society, as of the Gospel of Jesus Christ, is the quality of sharing gifts and challenges. Be assured of my prayers. I look forward to the outcomes as they emerge.

Another of our speakers represents the Methodist Church. Frances Young is a deeply grounded Methodist. Here in the United Kingdom,

Methodism's membership stands only at 188,000, but worldwide there are over eighty million Methodists. The secretary to the Methodist Conference, the Reverend Canon Gareth Powell, sent us this:

> Please convey my best wishes and the assurance of my prayers to all gathered at the "Inspiring Service" panel. I was delighted to have this opportunity to reflect on vocation and Christian service, particularly in the light of the Methodist Church's graduate development programme, now in its second year, which seeks to provide young people with opportunities to spend a year exploring faith alongside a paid placement with a range of professional organizations from Action for Children to the House of Lords. The Methodist Church affirms repeatedly its belief that the ministry of the people of God in the world is both the primary and normative ministry of the Church and that it is in the context of the world that God so loves that we live out our calling. I am sure that the conversation on Friday and the commitment to deeper mutual understanding that it represents will be both fruitful and engaging. I do hope you have a profitable day, and I will be interested to hear more of the venture, which seems to be addressing a particularly pressing challenge.

We ponder, then, at the outset just for a moment, the faith communities represented by our four speakers here tonight. Add up these communities, and it comes to about 1.4 billion people worldwide, which sets our western European experience of faith in decline in dramatic context. Now we are not in the numbers game per se, but if we also consider the evidence of the disproportionately positive impact upon voluntary contributions to society that people of faith make, we can see a significant counter to a depressed evaluation of the "place" of faith communities and their impact on our world.

Now to introduce our speakers. First is David, Lord Alton, a senior lay Catholic, very active in the political life of the nation and the world. Lord Alton is a former Liberal Party and later Liberal Democrat Member of Parliament, who has sat as a cross-bench member of the House of Lords since 1997. He is known very much for his human rights work, including the co-founding of Jubilee Action, the children's charity now known as Chance for Childhood. He is also Professor of Citizenship at Liverpool John Moores University, but more importantly (to this College), he is father of Marianne, who studied philosophy and theology here with excellence, energy, joy, and wit and who is now a barrister spending much of her year doing pro bono work in Uganda.

Elder Jeffrey R. Holland is here with his wife, Sister Patricia Holland. He was ordained a member of the Quorum of the Twelve Apostles of The Church of Jesus Christ of Latter-day Saints in 1994. He was the ninth president of Brigham Young University, so he serves both in the faith community and the academy. He was president of the American Association of Presidents of Independent Colleges and Universities, among many other things, and is known for his work with understanding communities that are being persecuted, especially Christians and Jews (he was given a Torch of Liberty for that work), and supporting the plight of dispossessed and refugee communities, such as the Yazidis.

Rowan, Lord Williams is a Welsh Anglican bishop, theologian, poet, and was the 104th Archbishop of Canterbury, Metropolitan of the Province and Primate of all England, and leader as First Among Equals of the Anglican community worldwide from 2003 until 2012. Previously, he was Bishop of Monmouth and Archbishop of Wales and Regius Professor of Divinity and Canon of Christ Church, Oxford. He is now Master of Magdalen College in Cambridge.

The Reverend Professor Frances Young taught theology at the University of Birmingham from 1971 to 2002. She was Edward Cadbury Professor and head of the Department of Theology, Dean of the Faculty of Arts, and Pro-Vice-Chancellor. She is also an ordained Methodist minister, which allows her to serve and preach in a deprived and formerly industrial Methodist circuit of the West Midlands—the so-called Black Country—while still pursuing her academic service. She preached at the opening ceremony of the eighth General Synod of the Church of England and was the first Methodist and the first woman to preach at the Eucharist at which Archbishop Rowan presided. She writes about Christianity in its formative centuries, as well as about the New Testament. Additionally, she has reflected publicly, at personal cost, upon her experience of being the mother of Arthur, her firstborn son who was born with profound disabilities. For this reason, she has worked on the theological and ecumenical dimensions of L'Arche communities and the Faith and Light movement with Canadian Catholic philosopher, theologian, and humanitarian Jean Vanier. Her drawing room also bears photographic witness that, I think in 1965, she was the first woman to climb the mountain Ranrapalca in the Peruvian Andes.

Without further ado, ladies and gentlemen, we look forward to hearing about "Inspiring Service" from them.

Notes

[1] Thanks were offered at this point to members of the college who had helped significantly with arranging the event and dinner, among them Lara Avincola, Kevin Dudley, Chris Long, and their departments for their labour and support.

David Alton

Receiving an invitation from Andrew Teal is a bit like a three-line whip—not least because of the debt I owe him for the kindness and inspiration he showed my daughter when she was here as a student. I have drawn the short straw for alphabetical reasons, so I'm the warm-up act for my colleagues who will follow.

Only in Britain would the words community service be turned into a punishment to be dispensed by the courts. The principle of serving others is a central tenet of citizenship; for Christians, it is at the very heart of the gospel; the service of others changes lives, changes society, and changes us—all for the better. It is the animating principle for public life par excellence.

It draws its force from the recognition that every human person (every soul) is worth more than the whole of the rest of the created order—each unique, each a person made in the image and likeness of God, each with inherent dignity and worth, and each made to express themselves as moral beings that grow in love and charity through their own particular gifts.

I have assumed that when Andrew sent me the examination topic, "Inspiring Service—Discuss", he would want me to reflect on the almost forty years spent in Parliament and the eight years before that when I served an inner-city neighbourhood in Liverpool, where half the homes had no inside sanitation and where I was elected, while I was a final-year student, as a city councillor.

Let me follow the example of the Romans who divided Gaul into three parts: firstly, what principles should inspire service through politics; secondly, how faith should inspire us to serve; and thirdly, who has inspired me—principles, practice, people.

What principles should inspire service through politics?
Every day that I am at Westminster, I walk through Westminster Hall, where Parliament first met in 1265, where Thomas More and Charles I were tried, and where, in 1965, Winston Churchill was laid in state.

As a young boy, along with millions of others, I walked past Churchill's coffin. He has been lionized as the man who saved democracy. Yet Churchill had a realistic view of democracy and politics, once saying:

> Many forms of Government have been tried, and will be tried in this world of sin and woe. No one pretends that democracy is perfect or all-wise. Indeed, it has been said that democracy is the worst form of Government except for all those other forms that have been tried from time to time.[1]

This least "worst form of Government" in this "world of sin and woe"—impaired but always preferable to dictatorship or totalitarianism—cannot function without virtue, commonly held values, and a belief in serving the nation rather than serving yourself or serving sectional interests.

In 1979, elected to the House of Commons, I was privileged to serve alongside the last members who had seen active service in the Second World War and who had served alongside Churchill in the House. Overwhelmingly, regardless of their party allegiances, they believed in public service and the principle of duty.

The alternative approach to political service can be found in Niccolò Machiavelli's *The Prince*. He tells us that the ruler should be prepared to choose evil as the price of power and not hesitate to deceive. Mercifully, he didn't have access to Twitter. Machiavelli despised many traditional Christian beliefs and turned words such as virtue on their heads, believing that real virtue emanated from the pursuit of ambition, glory, and power.

And of course, this represented a fundamental break with Thomas Aquinas, medieval scholasticism, and the Aristotelian belief in the principle and pursuit of virtue. Aristotle had a high view of the polis. He insisted that "we are not solitary pieces in a game of chequers" but all players in a common life and that "*aidos*—shame—would attach to the citizens who refused to play their part".[2] Aristotle warned that "he that is incapable of society, or so complete in himself as not to want it, makes no part of a city, as a beast or a god".[3] Aquinas echoed Aristotle in extolling the cardinal virtues of prudence, justice, temperance, and courage. This inspired belief in the value of virtuous service is captured in many societies and systems of belief.

My mother was a native Irish speaker from the west of Ireland. On the wall of the council flat where I grew up, we had some words in Irish which, translated, said, "It is in the shelter of each other's lives that the people live".

We lived next door to a Jewish lady, Sadie Moonshine, who would have been familiar with Hillel's admonition "If I'm not for myself who will be? But if I am only for myself, who am I?"[4]

Nelson Mandela often reflected on the idea of Ubuntu—a person is a person because of other people. Archbishop Desmond Tutu explained, "A person with Ubuntu is open and available to others . . . and is diminished when others are humiliated or diminished, when others are tortured or oppressed."[5] Ubuntu is only possible in a person with this common good mentality, a mentality at odds with our cold, calculated, utilitarian, social mores.

Public policy can never be legitimate if it does not serve and promote the flourishing of each unique, created person and withstand the violation of a minority or even a single individual because there can be no common good that does not respect our equal worth and dignity first.

We don't exist, then, in isolation; we are not simply individuals who, in a parody of the gospel, think it is okay to "do unto others before they do you" and demand bigger, faster, better, more, and the absolute right to choose while being oblivious to the consequences on others.

The great nineteenth-century idealist and exponent of ethical liberalism, and indeed of Oxford, City Councillor Thomas Hill Green was right when he said, "If the idea of the community of good for all men has even now little influence, the reason is that we identify the good too little with good character and too much with good things."[6]

The concept that we should place ourselves at the service of others—at the service of the common good and at the service of the weakest, the poorest, the most vulnerable—gives form and expression to the desire of the virtuous citizen to generously and altruistically use their privileges and their talents in the inspired service of others.

But, friends, a snapshot of contemporary Britain shows what happens when we stop looking out for others, where toxic loneliness replaces family and community cohesion and too many feel like losers even when they are thought to be winners in purely material terms and where without shared values and rules, stable relationships, a sense of duty, and a willingness to serve others, we too easily shrink into merely atomized individuals, invariably unhappy, unfulfilled, and often alone.

Whether we like it or not, we come from a community, with all its faults and failings, and each of us, with all our own faults and failings, do have some gift to return. That's how it should be.

But too often, regrettably, public service through politics has been replaced by a self-serving and self-regarding form of careerism too often dominated by attempts to climb Disraeli's greasy pole; too often characterized by growing intolerance and toxicity, reflected even at universities like this one, with the disallowance of platforming alternative views; too often governed by narrow ideologies, increasingly disconnected from communities, creating a vacuum into which organizations with extreme and inflammatory views are able to enter with ease.

Gandhi warned of the danger of becoming disconnected: "To forget how to dig the earth and to tend the soil is to forget ourselves", telling us, "You must be the change you want to see in the world."[7]

If we want to change the world, we need to change our nation; if we want to change our nation, we have to change our communities; if we want to change our communities, we change our families; and if we want to change our families, we have to change ourselves. Change doesn't come about by itself; it comes through active participation and voluntary service. Sometimes that will be through elected office. Desmond Tutu, an African Anglican bishop, once said that politics is not a dirty business—just that some of the players have dirty hands, and he was right. Politics are ultimately only as good as the people who are engaged with them. And what happens when democracy is hollowed out?

The year 2017 saw the centenary of the Bolshevik Revolution, which paved the way for totalitarianism, social engineering, state terror, and mass murder, leaving a legacy of prison camps and unmarked graves. Thirty million people were executed, starved to death, or perished in labour camps in what was the bloodiest century in human history, with the loss of a hundred million lives. The century began with the Armenian genocide and culminated in the Holocaust and the depredations of the four mass murderers of the twentieth century: Mao, Stalin, Hitler, and Pol Pot.

Our former chief rabbi Jonathan Sacks reminds us, "Do not ask 'Where was God at Auschwitz?', ask, 'Where was man?'"[8] The great Protestant theologian Dietrich Bonhoeffer warned each of us, "Not to speak is to speak; and not to act is to act."[9]

Does faith inspire us to serve?
If all of this should guide us into political service, what does the Christian faith say to us?

Every person uniquely reflects the divine likeness, and for that reason alone we are required to uphold the dignity of each. In rendering unto Caesar, we don't need to stop seeing everything through the lens of our faith.

When Churchill, who was not known for religious ardour, was once described as "a pillar of the church", he corrected the speaker by interjecting that he was "not a pillar, but a buttress, supporting it from outside."[10] And why? Churchill insisted, "The flame of Christian ethics is still our highest guide. Only by bringing it into perfect application can we hope to solve for ourselves the problems of this world and not of this world alone."[11] Churchill understood that the least "worst form of government" was dependent on Judaeo-Christian values and ideals.

And if he was our greatest twentieth-century prime minister, surely Mr. William Ewart Gladstone was the greatest of the nineteenth century. Gladstone said this: "As to its politics, this country has much less, I think, to fear than to hope; unless through a corruption of its religion—against which, as Conservative or Liberal, I can perhaps say I have striven all my life."[12] This is a sentiment which surely William Wilberforce, Lord Shaftesbury, Keir Hardie, and many other significant political figures would have conferred. In an inspiring letter, in fact the last he wrote, John Wesley told Wilberforce to use all his political skills to end slavery and to fight for human dignity, warning that:

> unless the divine power has raised you up to be as Athanasius contra mundum, I see not how you can go through your glorious enterprise in opposing that execrable villainy which is the scandal of religion, of England, and of human nature. Unless God has raised you up for this very thing, you will be worn out by the

opposition of men and devils. But if God be for you, who can be against you? Are all of them together stronger than God? O be not weary of well doing! Go on, in the name of God and in the power of his might, till even American slavery (the vilest that ever saw the sun) shall vanish away before it.[13]

In all our faith traditions, we need to encourage greater emphasis, then, on an outpouring of service, including into politics. And what a blessing this can be. After all, 84 per cent of the world's population is religious.

From the Catholic tradition, where do I look for inspiration?

Well, John Henry Newman told his Oxford students to love their country and to serve the nation: "We are not born," he said, "for ourselves, but for our kind, for our neighbours, for our country: it is but selfishness, indolence, a perverse fastidiousness, an unmanliness, and no virtue or praise, to bury our talent in a napkin."[14]

Jacques Maritain, in *Integral Humanism*, asserted, "Christianity taught men that love is worth more than intelligence,"[15] insisting that Christianity may not need democracy to survive but that democracy needs Christianity if it is to thrive.

Democracy isn't a spectator sport; Christians must offer servant leadership and fearlessly champion human dignity.

G. K. Chesterton, writing in 1930, said, "When people begin to ignore human dignity, it will not be long before they begin to ignore human rights."[16]

The Church fathers say the same, declaring in 1965 in *Dignitatis Humanae* that "religious freedom therefore ought to have this further purpose and aim, namely, that men may come to act with greater responsibility in fulfilling their duties in community life".[17] In *Veritatis Splendor*, in 1993, they state, "As history demonstrates, a democracy without values easily turns into an open or thinly disguised totalitarianism."[18] In 2009, in *Caritas in Veritate*, referred to earlier, it declares, "Many people . . . are concerned only with their rights. Hence it is important to call for a renewed reflection on how rights presuppose duties, if they are not to become mere license."[19] And Pope Francis, in 2016, in *The Name of God Is Mercy*, rebukes those who neglect love, using the metaphor of the church as a field hospital rather than a perfected society—where we who are the most wounded can encounter Christian love in action.[20] Inspiring and channelling adherents into public service is then transformative of individuals and society.

Who has inspired me?

So much for the principles and practice. What about the people? Never forget the local councillors, the political activists, and the backroom people who organize elections and the unsung and unseen heroes who spend hour after hour in advice centres and hospitals dealing with day-to-day crises and problems facing constituents and also demonstrating that they genuinely care about individuals.

I have a poster on my study wall that says "God so loved the world, he did not send a committee". Part of what you have to do if you're going to be involved in any kind of service is to navigate committees and spend hours and hours in them.

In a great book called *Two Cheers for Democracy*, E. M. Forster described a liberal who has found liberalism crumbling beneath him but insisted that the idiosyncratic, bloody-minded, back-bench member of Parliament who gets some minor injustice put right is the justification of our imperfect system of democracy.[21]

Well, inspired political service can put right more than minor injustices. I have mentioned Wilberforce, who with Clarkson, the Quaker ladies, and others campaigned for forty years against the slave trade. And think of heroes like Dietrich Bonhoeffer or Maximilian Kolbe, whose stand against Nazism cost them their lives.

But there are countless others, too, who should inspire us to use the gifts we have been given. As a teenager, I was inspired by Robert Kennedy and Dr Martin Luther King—both murdered for their beliefs. Kennedy insisted that "each of us can work to change a small portion of events".[22]

Last month I was in Pakistan raising the case of Asia Bibi—an illiterate woman who worked in the fields nine years ago and was given a death sentence for so-called, alleged blasphemy. And recently you will have read she has been acquitted of those charges but is still not free to leave that country.

In 2011, after championing her case, the Christian minister for minorities, Shahbaz Bhatti, and the Muslim governor of the Punjab,

Salmaan Taseer, were both murdered: Bhatti said this just months before his death: "I know the meaning of the Cross. I am following the Cross, and I am ready to die for a cause." [23]

Esther famously said, "If I perish, I perish," for "how can I bear to see the calamity that is coming on my people?" (Esther 4:16; 8:6).

Asia Bibi, like Bhatti, like Salmaan Taseer, like Esther, came into the world, again in words from the book of Esther, "for just such a time as this" (Esther 4:14). Shahbaz Bhatti's murderers have never been brought to justice, whilst last year a mob of 1,200 people forced two children to watch as their Christian parents were burned alive. Think, too, of the twenty-one Coptic Christians who, in 2015, in the moment of their barbaric execution by ISIS were repeating the words "Lord Jesus Christ", or of the two North Korean women who appeared before a committee chair and described egregious and brutal violations of human rights.

Friends, when you encounter people facing murder, beheadings, rape, terror, and intimidation, you can feel overawed but inspired too.

These examples and these stories are pointless unless they inspire us to do something about it—to put our array of amazing gifts and privileges at the service of others.

In these three points—principles, addressing the principles that should inspire service through politics; practice, stating how faith should inspire us to serve; and people, mentioning some of those who have inspired me—I hope that I have at least done a little bit of justice to Andrew's challenge to reflect tonight on inspiring service. Thank you.

Notes

1. Winston Churchill, "The Worst Form of Government", International Churchill Society, <https://winstonchurchill.org/resources/quotes/the-worst-form-of-government/>, accessed 14 August 2020.
2. David Alton, review of *The Political Animal: An Anatomy*, by Jeremy Paxman, *Third Way* 26:2 (March 2003), p. 28.
3. Aristotle, *A Treatise on Government*, trans. William Ellis (London: George Routledge and Sons, 1888), p. 13.
4. R. Hillel the Elder, *Pirke Avot* I.14, trans. Charles Taylor, <https://sacred-texts.com/jud/sjf/sjf03.htm>, accessed 14 August 2020. Compare Primo Levi's 1982 novel *Se Non Ora, Quando?*
5. Desmond Tutu, quoted in "Mission and Philosophy", Desmond Tutu: Peace Foundation, <http://www.tutufoundationusa.org/desmond-tutu-peace-foundation/>, accessed 14 August 2020.
6. Thomas Hill Green, *Prolegomena to Ethics*, ed. A. C. Bradley (Oxford: Clarendon Press, 1906), p. xxix.
7. Mahatma Gandhi, *The Collected Works of M. K. Gandhi* (New Delhi, India: Publications Division, 1960), 13:241. "We but mirror the world. If we could change ourselves, the tendencies in the world would also change. As a man changes his own nature, so does the attitude of the world change towards him. This is the divine mystery supreme. We do not need to want to see what others do."
8. Rabbi Lord Jonathan Sacks said, "The question that haunts me after the Holocaust, as it does today in this new age of chaos, is 'Where is man?'" "The Faith of God" (*Bereishit* 5778), The Office of Rabbi Sacks, 10 October 2017, <https://rabbisacks.org/faith-god-bereishit-5778/>, accessed 14 August 2020.
9. Attributed to Bonhoeffer by Eric Metaxas, *Bonhoeffer: Pastor, Martyr, Prophet, Spy* (Nashville: Thomas Nelson, 2010); though it is claimed to be a hyperbolic metaphor on Twitter, 22 May 2016.
10. Richard Langworth, "Churchill on Britain and Europe: A Pillar or a Buttress?," *American Spectator*, 11 July 2017, <https://spectator.org/churchill-on-britain-and-europe-a-pillar-or-a-buttress/>, accessed 14 August 2020.
11. Winston Churchill, "The 20th Century—Its Promise and Its Realization" (MIT Mid-Century Convocation, Boston, 31 March 1949), in *Winston*

Churchill: His Complete Speeches, 1897–1963, ed. Robert Rhodes James (New York: Chelsea House, 1974), vol. 7, pp. 7807ff.

12   William Ewart Gladstone, quoted in J. P. Parry, *Democracy and Religion: Gladstone and the Liberal Party, 1867–1875* (Cambridge: Cambridge University Press, 1986), p. 451.

13   John Wesley to William Wilberforce, 24 February 1791.

14   John Henry Newman, "The Present Position of Catholics in England" (lecture, Birmingham, 1851).

15   Jacques Maritain, "Rights of Man and Natural Law, The Person and the Common Good, Christianity and Democracy, Man and the State", chapter 13 of *The Collected Works of Jacques Maritain* (Notre Dame, IN: University of Notre Dame Press, 1996), Internet edition, <https://maritain.nd.edu/jmc/jmworks.htm>, accessed 14 August 2020.

16   Lawrence J. Clipper (ed.), *The Collected Works of G. K. Chesterton* (San Francisco: Ignatius Press), vol. 35, p. 306.

17   "Declaration on Religious Freedom *Dignitatis Humanae* on the Right of the Person and of Communities to Social and Civil Freedom in Matters Religious Promulgated by His Holiness Pope Paul VI On December 7, 1965", The Holy See, <http://www.vatican.va/archive/hist_councils/ii_vatican_council/documents/vat-ii_decl_19651207_dignitatis-humanae_en.html>, accessed 14 August 2020.

18   *Veritatis Splendor*, The Holy See, <http://www.vatican.va/content/john-paul-ii/en/encyclicals/documents/hf_jp-ii_enc_06081993_veritatis-splendor.html>, accessed 14 August 2020.

19   "Encyclical Letter *Caritas In Veritate* of the Supreme Pontiff Benedict XVI to the Bishops, Priests, and Deacons, Men and Women Religious, the Lay Faithful, and All People of Good Will on Integral Human Development in Charity and Truth", The Holy See, <http://w2.vatican.va/content/benedict-xvi/en/encyclicals/documents/hf_ben-xvi_enc_20090629_caritas-in-veritate.html>, accessed 14 August 2020.

20   Pope Francis, "Address of His Holiness Pope Francis to Representatives of Different Religions" (Clementine Hall, Rome, Thursday, 3 November 2016), <http://w2.vatican.va/content/francesco/en/speeches/2016/november/documents/papa-francesco_20161103_udienza-interreligiosa.html>, accessed 14 August 2020.

21   E. M. Forster, *Two Cheers for Democracy* (London: Penguin, 1965), p. 83.

22 "Bobby Kennedy Made This Speech to the Young People of South Africa on Their Day of Affirmation in 1966", <https://www.jfklibrary.org/learn/about-jfk/the-kennedy-family/robert-f-kennedy/robert-f-kennedy-speeches/day-of-affirmation-address-university-of-capetown-capetown-south-africa-june-6-1966>, accessed 14 August 2020.

23 Reported in "Profile", *Dawn Newspaper*, 2 March 2011

Jeffrey R. Holland

Lord Alton, thank you for that definitive statement. It was good fortune beyond the alphabet that had you lead off with that message. I'm grateful to Andrew Teal, my distinguished colleagues, and all of you for the invitation to be here. I'm a token on this programme for more reasons than one: I'm the token Yank from across the pond, and in a sense I'm the token representative of an institution that has not only given service but also received service and survived through the service, compassion, and charity of others.

We in The Church of Jesus Christ of Latter-day Saints have the questionable distinction of being the only church in the history of the United States of America to have an extermination order issued against it. That was a century and a half ago, but we have not forgotten that, and we've been very grateful to those who were willing, kind, compassionate— interested and responsible enough—to have helped us then. We've since spent a century and a half trying to do our best at helping others. So thank you for letting me represent a rather unique view from among those on our panel here; I certainly look forward to Lord Williams's and Reverend Young's messages to come.

The character of the giver

An act of service will not necessarily define the life or reveal the character of the recipient. It might, but it wouldn't necessarily do so. But I do believe that it will almost always define the life and reveal the character of the giver, and it's against that context that I wish to talk a little bit about the New Testament context for the kind of service that Lord Alton so brilliantly described here in a contemporary way.

In what would probably be the most startling moment of His early ministry, Jesus stood up in his home synagogue in Nazareth and read these words prophesied by Isaiah and recorded in the Gospel of Luke: "The Spirit of the Lord is upon me, because he has anointed me to bring good news to the poor. He has sent me to proclaim release to the captives . . . to let the oppressed go free" (Luke 4:18). Thus, the Saviour made the first public announcement of his messianic ministry. But this verse also made clear that on the way to his ultimate atoning sacrifice and Resurrection, Jesus's first and foremost messianic duty would be to bless others, "succor the weak, lift up the hands which hang down, and strengthen the feeble knees" (*Doctrine and Covenants* 81:5). James called such care for others "the royal law" (James 2:8)—his synonymous title of the second great commandment. Paul wrote to the Galatians that "the whole law is summed up in a single commandment, 'You shall love your neighbour as yourself'" (Galatians 5:14). Christ's ministry and his teachings leave no room to doubt the seriousness with which we must embrace this sacred instruction—to inspire service and to serve inspiringly. Certainly, he so served and so inspired.

In the process of teaching this principle, he gave what is arguably the most renowned and oft quoted parable in the New Testament canon. When asked, "Who is my neighbour?" (Luke 10:29), Jesus told the story the whole Western world has come to know—that of a man travelling from Jerusalem to Jericho who fell among thieves and was wounded, robbed, and left at the wayside to die. A priest and a Levite came by and looked on him and passed by on the other side. Into this scene then came a Samaritan, a man to whose people and cities the Twelve had been forbidden to go. This otherwise unworthy man stopped and gave immediate aid to the troubled one, then arranged for his continuing care at a nearby inn. To his inquirer, Jesus then asked, "'Which of these three, do you think, was a neighbour to the man who fell into the hands of the robbers?' He said, 'The one who showed him mercy.' Jesus said to him, 'Go and do likewise.'" (Luke 10:36–37).

Inspiring service—it would be difficult not to see the vital role such care for others plays in the very fundamentals of Christian faith. Jesus, in his life and teachings, made it clear that caring for others was not an option. Indeed, he declared that without it one could not qualify for the greatest of eternal blessings—eternal life. The scriptures consistently teach that acts of Christian service are expressions of Christian love.

Adversity is all around us. It's all about us; it's among us on every side, or so it seems. Some of it is man-made. Some of it comes from natural forces, but whatever the source, adversity and trial are inevitable elements of mortality, and ultimately all of us have some confrontation with it. But our religion, centring on the life and mission of the Lord Jesus Christ, helps us comprehend that. We comprehend that God and Christ love us with a mature, perfect love. Furthermore, in an effort to counter earthly ills that strike us, they call the members of our earthly family to be instruments of their love and "doers of the word" (James 1:22). So we have the great honour to be invited to be these instruments for inspiring service. We need God, but he also needs us. It's an inspiring thought to think that not only humankind but divinity itself needs our heart and needs our helping hand. Surely that must be one way that we are heirs of God and joint heirs with Christ (see Romans 8:17).

Quiet, unheralded service
Another thought that makes such service inspiring is that it's often done in demonstrated obscurity—in quiet rooms, in homes and hospitals and places of confinement, in prisons and refugee camps and residential centres for the elderly—many, many places far from the public eye. Usually it's unheralded, but ironically, it reflects the very public standard set by the Saviour for those who will inherit the kingdom prepared from the foundation of the world. These are they who serve the hungry, the thirsty, the naked, the homeless, and those who are sick, or in prison, or in pain. They do all of this after the pattern and in the spirit of him who said "Just as you did it to one of the least of these who are members of my family, you did it to me" (Matthew 25:40). Conversely, to those who fail to minister to the needy, he said, "Just as you did not do it to one of the least of these, you did not do it to me" (Matthew 25:45).

May I refer to a first-century BC incident in the New World, recorded in our Book of Mormon: Another Testament of Jesus Christ? There the prophet Alma urged his congregation to cry to the Lord over all their activities and all their possessions, all their flocks and all their fields, and for the general welfare of themselves and those about them (see Alma 34:17–27). Their whole attitude was to be one of prayerful gratitude to the Lord for all that they had been given and all that they were blessed with. Then Alma said rather sternly, "Do not suppose that this is all; for after ye have done all these things"—that is, been prayerfully thankful for all that we have been given—"if ye turn away the needy, and the naked, and visit not the sick and afflicted, and impart of your substance, if ye have, to those who stand in need—I say unto you, if ye do not any of these things, behold, your prayer is vain, and availeth you nothing, and ye are as hypocrites who deny the faith" (Alma 34:28).

The impact of one person

Given the monumental challenge of addressing immense need in the world, what can one man or one woman do? The Master himself offered an answer. When before his betrayal and crucifixion Mary anointed Jesus's head with an expensive burial ointment, Judas Iscariot protested this extravagance and murmured against her. Jesus said, "Why do you trouble her? She has performed a good service for me. She has done what she could" (Mark 14:6,8). "She has done what she could"—what a succinct formula!

A journalist once questioned Mother Teresa about her hopeless task of rescuing the destitute of Calcutta. He said that, statistically speaking, she was accomplishing absolutely nothing. This remarkable little woman shot back that her work was not about statistics—it was about love. Notwithstanding the staggering number beyond her reach, she said she could keep the commandment to love God and her neighbour by serving those who were within her reach with whatever resources she had. "What we do is nothing but a drop in the ocean," she would say on another occasion, "but if we didn't do it, the ocean would be one drop less than it is."[1] Soberly, the journalist concluded that Christianity is obviously not a statistical endeavour. He reasoned that if there would be more joy in heaven over one sinner who repents than over the ninety and nine who need no repentance, then apparently God is not overly preoccupied with percentages either.[2] In poetic form, we're hard-pressed to improve on the prayer often attributed to Saint Ignatius Loyola: "To give and not to count the cost, to fight and not to heed the wounds, . . . to labour and not to look for any reward, save that of knowing that I do your holy will."[3] Jesus did not just speak about love; He showed it virtually every hour of his life. He did not take himself away from the crowd, at least not permanently. He constantly returned to the people, even after his prayer, looking for the child, the publican, the suffering woman, the anguished man who needed him. He didn't just teach a Sabbath class about reaching out in love and then delegate the actual work to those in the audience. No, it was always "Come, follow me" (Matthew 19:21). Come, do as I do. "Take up [your] cross, and follow me. For those who want to save their life will lose it, and those who lose their life for my sake [in keeping the royal law] will find it" (Matthew 16:24–25).

One of the New Testament teachings that inspires service in me are these lines from Matthew 9: "When he saw the crowds, he had compassion for them, because they were harassed and helpless, like sheep without a shepherd. Then he said to his disciples, 'The harvest is plentiful, but the labourers are few; therefore ask the Lord of the harvest to send out labourers into his harvest.'" (Matthew 9:36–38).

The fact of the matter is true love requires action. We can speak of love all day long, we can write notes and sonnets that proclaim it, we can sing lyrics that praise it, and we can preach sermons that encourage it, but until we manifest that love in action our words are nothing. No, they are actually something: "a noisy gong" and "a clanging cymbal" (1 Corinthians 13:1). "Love never ends. But as for prophecies, they will come to an end; as for tongues, they will cease; as for knowledge, it will come to an end" (1 Corinthians 13:8). We have the message of the New Testament and the testimony of the Lord Jesus Christ to encourage our pursuit of inspiring service. May we do so even more successfully as a result of tonight's conversation.

Notes

[1] *Mother Teresa of Calcutta, My Life for the Poor*, ed. José Luis González-Balado and Janet N. Playfoot (San Francisco: Harper & Row, 1985), p. 20.

[2] See Malcolm Muggeridge, *Something Beautiful for God: Mother Teresa of Calcutta* (New York: Harper & Row, 1986), pp. 28–29, 118–19.

[3] Jack Mahoney, SJ, "A Mysterious Ignatian Prayer", *Thinking Faith*, blog, 17 February 2012, <https://thinkingfaith.org/articles/20120217_1.htm>, accessed 14 August 2020; see also J. Munitiz, SJ, "A Pseudo-Ignatian Prayer", *Letters and Notices* 97:426 (Autumn 2004), pp. 12–14.

Rowan Williams

It's a very great honour and pleasure to be alongside such a distinguished panel this evening and to have a chance to reflect for a few minutes on what constitutes service and why it's part of our essential humanity.

Not so very long ago, there died in this country a very remarkable and influential philosopher who was much underrated in the Christian community for many years. Her name was Mary Midgley, and one of the books, which she published about fifteen years ago, was under the title of *The Myths We Live By*, a powerful collection of essays looking at the various comforting fictions we tell ourselves about our humanity in our current society. She was particularly concerned about the fictions we tell ourselves about the environment we live in and its apparent inexhaustibility. Long before green issues were as prominent as they now are, Mary Midgley was underlining them as issues of greatest moral significance. But also among the myths we live by, she was able to name the pervasive fiction that tells us that the fundamental form of human life is rivalry. Thanks to a particularly unintelligent reading of Charles Darwin, the notion that the survival of the fittest is the law of evolution has taken a powerful hold on the human imagination, especially in the Western world. But the story of evolution is in fact rather different from what that reading might suggest. The more complex carbon-based forms of life become, the more it seems they are interdependent: the more they need one another and the more cooperation, mutual assurance, nourishment, and protection actually come to matter. And to overcome the myth of individual rivalry as the basic form of life, we need a robust account of how advanced life forms, developed life forms, are interdependent.

To put it rather more concretely, we learn and we are fed. The first thing that happens to us as human beings is that we are fed and among the next things that happen to us is that we learn to communicate. We receive before we give. We are what we are quite literally because of what we receive, and in becoming givers ourselves, we fulfil our role within a complex, interdependent form of life. In Christian scripture, this is presented as the optimal form of our life. It is referred to metaphorically as the Body of Christ, in which each agent is given a gift to share with others and each agent needs to receive from others. Whenever you encounter another human subject, the questions you must ask are: What is the gift that they alone can give me, and what is the gift only I can give them? And so it is that the characteristic, distinctive, radical thing about human life is that we are the most complicatedly, sophisticatedly interdependent life-form that there is. To be human is to be inserted into that pattern of giving and receiving wherever we are and whoever we are.

That means, of course, that while we may quite rightly talk about altruism in the sense of putting somebody else's interests ahead of ours (and I know that Oxford is the home of the effective altruism school of ethics), nonetheless we shouldn't forget that there is something about our service of others that is quite simply the way we learn to exercise our humanity in its fullness. In other words, the self-interest of wanting to be myself most fully is, paradoxically, interest in learning how I'm most free to serve and to nourish my neighbour.

There's no great gulf between being selfish and unselfish here. If I want to be myself, that's how to do it. We get some glimpse of this, don't we, in those various forms of human activity that are necessarily and irreducibly shared if they're going to work at all. The devoted and gifted solo violinist who performs devotedly and giftedly as a soloist within an orchestra is not actually doing anything very much for herself or for the orchestra. There's a famous nineteenth-century novel about undergraduate life in Oxford, by somebody who had no idea at all about Oxford or undergraduate life, that contains a famous description of a boat race with the unforgettable attribution "All rowed fast, but none so fast as stroke."[1] That's the problem of individualism. You can't imagine a boat race without cooperative virtue; you can't imagine a choir or an orchestra without cooperative virtue. Being good at what you're doing is being good at the harmonics of that particular group and that shared activity whose goodness, whose excellence is all about how you learn to do it together. Your own excellence has to do with the attention, the careful listening, and the picking up of signals from those around you, enabling them to do what best they can.

So within the optimal human community, life circulates. What's good for me and what's good for you are at the end of the day going to be bound together, and one of those myths we live by, a myth which is perhaps unprecedentedly popular at the moment, is that there is some way of literally or metaphorically fencing off what's good for me so that it is completely irrelevant to what's good for you. I can keep myself safe and your security or your well-being are of no interest whatever to me.

At the same time as that particular toxic fiction gets a deeper and deeper hold on our world, we're also, strangely enough, becoming more and more aware of the way in which crises do not stop at borders, the way in which the suffering, the privation, and the challenges of communities on the other side of the globe become our issue very directly. We need as never before, I think, to challenge the inconsistency of a worldview that, in many ways, recognizes more fully our interdependence and an ethic that seems more and more to drift away from the ideas of common good and public service.

David began with three Ps—principles and practice and people. I'd like to add two more to that for discussion and reflection. One is an uncomfortable word—prophecy— uncomfortable because the prophetic tradition in the Jewish-Christian world is about challenging the myths we live by. Prophets in Hebrew scripture are those who above all challenge idolatry and unfaithfulness—that is, the worship of what is not ultimate as if it were ultimate and the betrayal of common virtue and commitment, mutual fidelity, and trustworthiness in society. And we're talking about service, so I hope we can talk about that prophecy as well: the capacity to challenge this particular fiction of idolatry and to name it for the nonsense it is.

The trouble is, though, that the word prophecy can come to sound a bit melodramatic. There's a part of most of us that would quite like to be prophetic, to stand up bravely in the public square and denounce manifest evils and then go home again and sleep well. The fact is that, again as David has indicated, and I think Frances will be underlining shortly, effective prophecy, like effective service in general, has a lot to do with the fifth P—prose. It's not all prophecy and it's not all poetry. Some of it is slog, boring, prosaic, routine work making tiny, but measurable, difference. And perhaps to phrase our thinking about service within a religious environment allows us to see that prose matters as much as prophecy or poetry; it allows us even to see that failure is not the end of the world.

We might almost add a sixth P—permission. Permission to fail. Permission not to solve everything. Permission not to be God, at the end of the day, which is the most liberating thing that can be said to any human being. We really don't have to be God because the job is taken. Others have spoken about particular examples and inspirations, and before I sit down, I want to mention one or two of the lives that have stirred and challenged me over the years. Some thirty years ago, my wife and I spent some time in southern Africa working for the Anglican Church there and had the great privilege of meeting a man named Beyers Naudé, a minister of the Dutch Reformed Church who had given up a promising career as a pastor in that church because he could no longer support the Dutch Reformed Church's attitude to apartheid. He preached a famous sermon in his large and successful church in Pretoria on the text "We Must Obey God Rather Than Man" and walked out of the church, resigning his office. My wife and I met him in very strange circumstances because he was at that moment under what was called a banning order. That is, he wasn't supposed to meet people, and if he was arranging to meet anybody, there had to be security people present, and he couldn't meet more than two people at once. So we met him in the lobby of a hotel in Johannesburg and conversed for an hour, which left a very deep mark, and as we parted I felt, as one sometimes does with great people, an urge to say something grateful to him, but I was very tongue-tied (you know how it is), and I found myself saying eventually, "I just need to say how very important you are to some of us." He smiled and said, "Well, you know, there's a point where you know they can't really touch you"—meaning that his integrity was so prosaic, so routine, he just got used to living in the light and didn't think he was doing anything particularly heroic.

But the second example is, to my mind, a story that tells us a little bit about what the prophetic might mean in certain contemporary circumstances. This is a story of somebody I met in Cambodia, introduced by a mutual friend, a few years ago in Phnom Penh. Scott Niessen, an Australian, had worked for some years in the media in the United States. He'd had some very highly placed jobs managing various projects in and around Hollywood. He serviced the needs and the careers of many quite famous household names and went on holiday one year to Cambodia, where he somehow or other managed to see something of the life of the children abandoned on the streets in Phnom Penh. As you may realize, Cambodia is a country still suffering the colossal trauma of the Khmer Rouge tyranny mentioned by David earlier. Generations were literally wiped out; broken families and parentless children are still a regular feature of life there. Scott spent some time simply getting to know something of the circumstances of the children living on the streets in the city from birth upward. He went back to the States and thought quite a lot about what he ought to do. Niessen went back to Phnom Penh to visit some of these communities in the streets again and to begin to work out what was the best thing that could be offered to them. He likes to tell the story of when he was there, walking through inches-deep sewage in the back streets of Phnom Penh with a couple of naked children clinging to his arms and legs, he had a call on his mobile phone. It was from one of his senior media clients in the United States, who wanted to complain to him that the video games on his private jet were not the ones that he'd ordered.

Scott says that that was the moment at which he realized what kind of human being he wanted to be and what kind of human being he didn't want to be. He gave up his job, he sold his house, he moved to Phnom Penh, and for the last eight years or so he has been running a charity in Phnom Penh that deals with nearly 1,500 children in the streets there. I had the privilege of spending a day with him, meeting some of the children he works with and seeing some of the work he does with the police in Phnom Penh. He's managed to persuade the police force in Australia to assist some people to the work in Phnom Penh so that they are able to train police there in safeguarding child protection: how to handle complaints of abuse, violence, and sexual exploitation. In other words, he's addressing both a personal and a structural set of problems, and he's one of those people who is very definitely among those who for me defines service and inspires because of that.

And the question that he found himself asking when he had that call on his mobile is the question that service finally prompts: what kind of human being do I want to be, and what kind of human being do I not want to be? Do I actually want to be part of that mutually nourishing humanity in which others' goodness actively feeds and enhances mine and my goodness actively feeds and enhances others, or do I want to be committed to a fiction that will, in the end, poison and kill us all? Thank you.

Notes

[1] Compare Desmond Francis Talbot Coke, *Sandford of Merton: A Story of Oxford Life* (Oxford, 1903), ch. 12, who likewise describes an individual rowing faster than his team: "His blade struck the water a full second before any other: the lad had started well. Nor did he flag as the race wore on. ... As the boats began to near the winning-post, his oar was dipping into the water nearly twice as often as any other."

Frances Young

In December 1974, at a secret location, some churchmen from Northern Ireland who were led by a Methodist minister met with the Provisional IRA Army Council to explore the possibility of a ceasefire. The IRA men arrived at a hotel in the remote village of Feakle, looked around, and asked the Methodist minister, "Who's that over there? He looks like an English colonel."

"He's the former headmaster of the Methodist College in Belfast," was the reply. "Would it help if I tell you he was a pacifist in the war?" The next morning it was him whom the IRA men accepted as chair of the talks.

Stanley Worrall was indeed an Englishman. He'd been headhunted in the early 1960s—the Methodist governors wanted a Methodist headmaster for their large co-educational grammar school. When he retired, he and his wife had stayed in Northern Ireland to contribute to public service and community work of various kinds. He was chair of the Northern Ireland Arts Council, and he served on the governing bodies of the Stranmillis (a teacher-training college), the then new University of Ulster at Coleraine, the Paddysburn Mental Hospital, and RTÉ (that's the Irish equivalent of the BBC) in Dublin.

He was my father. Most of my life I've recognized how living up to him shaped my career. He was an embodiment of the fact that Christianity is an intellectual tradition worthy of serious academic engagement and capable of making sense of life, the universe, and everything. He was a committed educationalist, passionate about forming the minds of young people. But I'm only now recognizing that it was his example of Christian commitment to public service that explains some of the odd decisions I made in the latter stages of my career.

When my family moved to Northern Ireland, I was already at university. I was about to take my classics finals, and I was trying to find ways of fulfilling a call to go on to study theology, to use my competence in Greek to study the New Testament. One Sunday, an elder statesman of Methodism came to address the Student Methodist Society. I asked him what place there was in Methodism for a woman theologian. "None," he said.

Nothing daunted, I went for my degree in theology. But then my life took an unexpected course: I married a scientist who was following a career in universities, and it made sense to follow him. In due time, we both landed jobs at the University of Birmingham. Meanwhile, long before the Anglicans, the Methodist Church had decided to ordain women and, somewhat out of the blue, in midlife, I had another call. Sometimes I speak, tongue in cheek, of my Damascus road experience, but that's another story.

So in 1984 I was ordained as a minister with permission to continue teaching theology at the university. Teaching has always been important to me—passing on what I've received and helping people to understand, to learn, to think. But my identity truly lies in being "a presbyter of the universal Church and one of John Wesley's preachers", as conveyed to me at my ordination retreat in 1984. There is nothing more profound and humbling as offering people what they need for their inner spiritual health, for their worship—placing the eucharistic elements in people's hands, speaking the word of God, and offering blessing.

So why on earth did I end up being a manager—head of department, Dean of Faculty, and Pro-Vice-Chancellor of the university? What were those years about? The question has never completely gone away. After all, most academics just want to get on with research and hate administration. Was it just ambition, nothing to do with—perhaps indeed contrary to—my Christian commitment?

It certainly was a response to the moral pressure of being the first woman to hold those positions: if one wasn't prepared to do it, how would things ever change?

But my ordination had taken place two years before; how did all that relate to ministry? At an overtly secular university, how could Christian commitment be expressed? What was I doing struggling with the frustrations of university politics? Practically everything I managed to achieve back then has by now been overtaken. There's no permanent legacy in running things day to day.

But I'm beginning to discern my debt to my father here too. The proper running of institutions is vitally important to society and crucial to facilitating people's flourishing. The endeavour to make the world a better place lies at the heart of the affirmation that this is God's world.

So now, in my own retirement, all that experience is feeding into another institutional commitment. I'm an elected public governor of the Birmingham Community Healthcare NHS Foundation Trust. The management board is accountable to us—the Council of Governors, volunteers who represent the public. And yes—it's frustratingly difficult to see what difference we make, the endless papers to be read, the data to be digested, and the meetings to go to don't always thrill me, to say the least. But the work of the trust really matters, and in using the skills I've acquired to act as a critical friend, I am giving back. For my own family has been, and doubtless will continue to be, beneficiaries of the services provided.

Which brings me to another crucial influence on who I am, what I think, what and who matters to me, and what I do, namely, my firstborn son, Arthur. Now fifty-one years old, he's entirely dependent on carers, has no self-help skills, no independent mobility, no language, and very little comprehension. We cared for him for forty-five years; he's now in residential care locally. The services of the NHS Community Trust have been, and still are, important in maintaining his life—the district nurses, the wheelchair service, physiotherapy, speech and language therapy (he has no language, but they provide the advice on his feeding and drinking), community dentistry, and, when he lived with us, the short-term respite service. That was our lifeline!

I could easily be distracted into talking about how I discovered the most fundamental human values in caring for Arthur—love, joy, peace, patience, kindness, faithfulness; Saint Paul lists nine of them and calls them the fruits of the Spirit (Galatians 5:22). Or I could tell how I found that it's in the struggles and darkness of human experience that one discovers the most meaningful gifts—sense and depth, grace and simplicity. But in this context Arthur's importance is in opening me up to people utterly different from myself and discovering how much the most unlikely people have to contribute.

All that was reinforced by my relationship with Jean Vanier, the founder of the L'Arche communities. From the organization's Roman Catholic roots, it is now an ecumenical, even multifaith, international organization, where barriers between people of utterly different backgrounds are dissolved by common commitment to those with learning disabilities, in the United States they call them developmental disabilities. Spiritual growth is discovered not only in the ups and downs of community life but in mutual relationships. That's the crucial point: so much service and charity work is top-down and patronizing, but at the heart of Jean Vanier's vision is the mutuality discovered in caring for those who cannot care for themselves: the assistants receiving unexpected gifts from those they assist, discovering things about themselves through the "other", the stranger, the one who's different.

Maybe that will strike you as a rather hackneyed, post-modern observation. But it's a truth I've also discovered in the multi-ethnic, inner-city churches I've served, where Arthur has always been part of my ministry.

And besides that, the discovery of this truth also came through the experience I gained from teaching theology to the pastors of black-led churches—an extramural programme set up by the University of Birmingham back in the 1980s. Oh yes, we began with profoundly different views of the Bible; from an academic perspective, they read scripture with a naive literalism. Yet their profound faith and hope, love and joy changed me. As a somewhat shy introvert, it was not always easy for me to reach out to those so different from myself, but I found a new freedom and, most important of all, discovered that you give people dignity by receiving from them. The most extraordinary moment came when some visitors to the course challenged the biblical criticism I was teaching, and the class leapt to my defence: "There are contradictions and difficulties in the Bible," they said, "and Frances is showing us how to understand them." We had grown together.

Preparing this for you has been important for my own self-understanding (and I'm afraid it has turned out to be something of a personal testimony—a good Methodist tradition, of course). By tradition, Methodists are activists. I've spent much of my life feeling guilty that I've done so little good in the world; I've not fed the hungry, healed the sick, welcomed the homeless, or visited those in prison. I've been one of a lucky generation: able to pursue my interests and, as a woman, have both a family and a career; I've never had to worry about mortgages or money or argue about them with my husband, without whose support and partnership I'd never have become what I am. He took early retirement to become Arthur's principal carer and treasurer of four different disability charities!

Yes, I've been lucky—so much luckier than my frustrated mother. Yet she modelled a constant search for vocation and a commitment to helping others, to the Methodist Church's healing ministry and to Girl Guides. And you have pushed me into reassessing my past. Through acknowledging even more comprehensively my need to live up to my father, I've reclaimed the importance of public service to secular institutions and grasped more of its theological grounding.

Reading the earliest Christian documents, both in and beyond the New Testament, what is striking is the claim of this little, underground (sometimes persecuted) group that their God is the God of the whole created order and that everybody is accountable to this God, who actually sees into the heart, knows the secrets of inner motivations, and expects everyone to do good, to be generous, and to live honourable lives, accepting the authority of human institutions: the pagan emperor himself was appointed by this one and only God to ensure justice and peace.

At this point in history, such subservience appears highly problematic, doesn't it? But, for all our current individualism, we are social animals; we need each other, and society still requires well-run institutions to govern competing interests, to ensure peace and justice, and to foster human flourishing in body, mind, and spirit.

The theological undergirding of public service is surely a commitment to the fact that this is God's world, despite the way things seem. It's been said that the Christian doctrine of sin (meaning not simply sex or individual misdemeanours, but rather the way human affairs in general keep going somewhat pear-shaped) is the only empirically grounded doctrine! Christian faith proclaims that God has taken action in Jesus Christ to put things right and calls us to play our part in that process. That's why commitment to making the world a better place lies at the heart of Christian service and why service means something other than imposing top-down control. It's no accident that humility and counting others more worthy than oneself has such prominence in the New Testament. We need people who are receptive to others to be the servants of all in our public life.

Questions and Responses

Teal: Thank you very much indeed for such diverse and inspiring addresses. I would like to sum up tonight by reflecting on who it is that can inspire others. It can seem, particularly with these stellar guests tonight, as if it is only the most articulate and powerful that inspire others, but I think I will share something with you, and I hope to spare someone's embarrassment.

I remember when I was eighteen years old I was sitting in a garden at Selly Park in Birmingham. I had prepared food for Arthur, of whom we have just heard, and one of the things he loved to do was throw his food on the floor after I had prepared it. It was a nice afternoon, we sat out in the garden. He was on his beanbag, and he had his rattle. The light was going through the trees and the way in which leaves fluttered made a beautiful pattern, and he was holding his hand out—I am not sure if he still does this?

Young: Yes!

Teal: There I was trying to read, trying so hard to read Karl Rahner and thinking, "I've had enough." And I looked at Arthur, and Arthur, without the din of words, in a sense, called me to be who I should be. One of the things about being human is our ability to be called out by another person, who in a sense calls us out into being. And actually that was a moment when I realized I do not need to be Karl Rahner; I do not need to be Frances Young, to do that profoundly. Arthur, by simply being himself and inhabiting who he was, had this immense way of inviting and challenging me to take my path. So thank you, panellists,

Arthur Young
(photo courtesy of Frances Young)

for sharing your vision and inspiration and for encouraging us to be who we are. Now, there's time for questions.

Question 1
Thank you so much for such an inspiring group of talks. Lord Alton, you mentioned that democracy without values quickly becomes a thinly disguised totalitarianism, which reminded me a lot of Walter Benjamin's idea that there is no document of civilization that is not the same as a document of barbarism and Theodor Adorno's idea that fascism is the aestheticization of politics. Lord Rowan, you also mentioned we need to challenge the inconsistency of our worldview, but Frances Young said we need to protect the nature of institutions.

I guess my question would be, how do we as Christians expand our empathic circle not just beyond the nation-state but to outside our species as well? For example, gorillas can speak two thousand words in the wild and can be taught; they have an IQ of eighty-nine. So philosophically defined, if not biblically defined, gorillas are persons, right? This example is just to illustrate my questions on how Christianity can help challenge our species' chauvinism, and what do we have to say about environmental civil disobedience? Could this be a form of service?

Alton: I've got the short straw again. I suppose, being at Oxford, I can quote C. S. Lewis, can't I? He was a member of the anti-vivisection society and once said, "If you start off being cruel to every other species, then you'll end up being cruel to your own."[1] Pope Francis writes (in *Laudato Si'*) about the entirety of creation and our duty to be good stewards of what God has given to us or entrusted to us, and I think that there is a real call in your generation, especially. Others in Rome have particularly referred to the way in which we have destroyed so much of what we have been given, and I think we will be held to account for much that we have done.

Your point about institutions is a good one as well because I think it was Thoreau who said that if you cut down all the trees, there'll be nowhere left for the birds to sing.[2] And it does worry me that we are at the point where so much of our institutional life in this country is under attack. I talk now again about politics for a moment, but we as political classes have a lot to answer for, specifically for what we have done to the institutions that have been entrusted to us. These are fragile things, and they are passed from generation to generation, and my theory is that it is the toxicity, the disconnection that I referred to earlier on, that is leaving people incredibly cynical with the political classes. I chaired one of the biggest meetings as a neutral chairman in the Brexit debate; I had my own views and cast my vote in the referendum like everyone else, but I was asked to chair a referendum meeting in Lancashire, and what struck me most about it was not how they voted, there was no doubt in my mind about how the people were going to vote (these were people from the Lancashire towns, places like Burnley, Blackburn, and Clitheroe), but it was the anger that was amongst the people there. They were not all racist and xenophobic people lining up behind the English Defence League. They were angry with politics and politicians, and they were going to give us all quite a kicking about the principal question that was going to be on the ballot paper in the referendum. So I think we have brought a lot of this on ourselves by the disassociation we have made with the people who are on the streets. Back in my parliamentary days, but even more so as a local councillor, we called it community politics. People will sometimes dismiss it as playing politics, but being there on the pavement, being there on the street, connecting with ordinary people, I think that there is a huge amount to be done to reclaim the lost ground. Because we do not do that, and there is a lot of cynicism about our institutions at this time, whether it is parliament, the Church, the broadcasting media, the law, and I think that's very dangerous for us.

Holland: In passing the microphone, I will just note that the adage is "think globally but act locally". The larger the institution, the greater the abstraction. Nevertheless, in the end, institutions are made up of people; they are made up of individuals, so I believe in a variation on that little theme: survey large fields but cultivate small ones. I do not know how else to deal with large institutions except to deal with the individuals in them. We should have what influence we can. Mother Teresa commented, "Do what you can", and that's usually not at a global level; it is not often at the institutional level. It is usually more private, more personal.

Williams: If I've got time for a very brief comment, first of all on gorillas and the like. Yes, I think the same fundamental principle applies: what is securing, nourishing for the environment we are in is bound up with what is secure for us, and the idea that the human race somehow lives six feet above the rest of the organic world is a myth. I think that is a key insight here, and I'm very glad you've underlined it so strongly. Which is also why, given the whole ecological picture, I have put my name to support the extinction rebellion in the last couple of weeks. But just very quickly on the word ecology—an ecology is a balanced, interactive system that finds equilibrium by the working of its components. That means that there's a social ecology as well. Part of a good social ecology is what I like to call sustainable institutions, that is, institutions that do not just wobble around depending on political fashion and electoral cycles. One of the biggest challenges we have is to create and maintain sustainable institutions—that is, institutions that have in view the good that is not just dictated by electoral cycles and political fashion. At the moment, we have been busy tearing up lots of those, or, as David just said, undermining them in various ways. Institutions need to think about how they regain and retain credibility because they have been guilty of betrayals and failures. And also I think we need to challenge the climate, the media climate of our society, which is hostile to institutions in problematic ways. So there is a lot, but ecology is the word I am coming back to here.

Young: Have you heard of slime mould? It is a living thing that is just one cell under normal circumstances, but in certain conditions the cells coalesce and you get what they call emergence. I think it was in 2004 that Japanese scientists said they taught slime mould to find the shortest route through a maze even though slime mould has no central nervous system, no brain, nothing. Now, I think that's a parable of the human race in relation to the planet. Actually one of the things that's really dangerous is the idea that we are single cells because corporately we do things through these sort of feedback mechanisms, influencing one another to the point where corporately we do things that are profoundly damaging to the very environment that sustains us. I think until we can start thinking through that, we are in a very dangerous place in terms of the future. But it's okay; I am not going to live much longer, you know. [laughter]

Question 2

My question is for Rowan Williams. I was really interested in your statement that advanced life forms are interdependent, and you think of the length of childhood, for different species, and human children are dependent for an awfully long time. As our world becomes more complex, perhaps that length of time is becoming even longer. So much of the scientific (and not just science but economics, evolutionary biology, and neurosciences) way of studying human nature is really from the point of view of the self. And there is sort of a selfishness in economic conceptions of rationality and the selfish gene, for example, in understanding how evolutionary biology works. It seemed to me in your comments there was a nascent theory of human character, of human identity, that was quite different from this emphasis on self and selfishness as being the key to understanding biology or human nature, economic relations, and so forth. I was wondering if you could just expand on that a little bit for us—and maybe even not just of human nature but of human ecology because that may tie in to the connectedness humans have to the environment and to other species . . .

Williams: Thank you, I won't try to give a lecture on the whole theory, you'll be glad to know. But I think one of the oddities of the last few decades is the eagerness with which people have embraced this mythology that I spoke about. And Richard Dawkins's selfish gene is not science; it's a massively inflated metaphor that is not recognized as such. I often like to say to secondary school students doing science, "Remember, there is no such thing as a gene. There's a little bloke in there." We talk about genes as a way of talking about the transmission of information, about intelligence.

As Frances was hinting, the whole ecology of creation, intelligence, the exchange of information, the feeding of systems into each other, feedback loops, all of that, that is the scientific world we are actually looking at these days—not this world of curious little chaps in armour going around inside us doing what they want, competing, and somehow winning little battles inside us. That's a bizarre picture, but whether it's neuroscience, evolutionary biology, or physics, the picture of unexpected, unplanned, and sometimes quite elusive connectedness is what the scientific world seems to be delivering to us now, and theology and philosophy really ought to be catching up with that. It's not to say that collectivities trump individualism; it's to say that relationship and intelligence are fundamental categories in the reality we experience. A lot more can be said, but that is where I would start.

Question 3

Everyone mentioned a bit about atomism in society, the breakdown of communities, and in a multicultural society here or anywhere in the Western world, how can we work against that if we insist on myths of Judaeo-Christian heritage? Rowan talked about prophecy and breaking down idolatry when the prophet who had the most to say about idolatry was Muhammad, and I am really struggling to see how Christianity or Judaism has more to say either in its history or in its philosophy about democracy over Islam. So, if we are living in a multicultural society and we are trying to break down barriers, how can we do that if we hold ourselves as the exemplar of what the right society should be, ourselves being the Christian community?

Young: I think I would come back to what I was saying about meeting the "other". What we need in our society is more people who reach out and meet the "others" who are different from themselves. It is when you actually receive from people who are different that you offer them dignity and become a part of a much larger whole. I do not think this can be done from the top down. I think it has to start with ordinary people in ordinary places who actually walk across the road that has become a barrier.

Williams: The last thing I would want to suggest is that somehow this is all about encouraging another round of Christian triumphalism. I am a Christian; I believe the Christian faith to be true; I believe that I can also learn from other religious traditions and that in the face of the kind of secularism that empties out the content from the world around us, we need to listen to one another and work together. So, to me, it is rather important that, as you rightly say, Islam is a tradition at the beginning of which is a rebellion against idolatry and that Buddhism is a tradition at the beginning of which is a rebellion against the idea of a solid, independent self. These are crucial insights that we need to save our world, as you might say. It does not alter the fact that, for me, the Christian faith is the most comprehensive and the most dependable picture of reality that I believe we can have. I will argue that with my Muslim and Buddhist friends till the cows come home. I do not expect them to agree overnight; I do not expect Christianity to be the dominant cultural presence in the world. I am grateful that there are other voices that echo back what I believe is most precious in my own legacy and enhance it in so echoing.

Holland: I don't think there would ever be a suggestion, certainly not from us and I do not think from any of you, that Christianity, the Judaeo-Christian tradition, or the Western world generally has some corner on the market of truth. We will be open to truth wherever it is and from whatever persuasion, whatever culture, whatever religious faith it comes from. That seems to me to be a given for contemporary issues, current social issues in the world in which we live. The advantage starts to come for Christians (as long as we are using that language and that persuasion tonight) and starts to take on its real significance, in another world. It is beyond the contemporary environment, contemporary ecology, that the real significance of Christianity and the life of Christ has its greatest meaning. So that takes it to a higher level for me when we talk about the distinctive quality and the unique characteristics of the Judaeo-Christian tradition. I would also say there are things that the Judaeo-Christian tradition brings to the contemporary world as well as the eternal one. However, not exclusively and not at the expense of others who also so teach. For example, when we talk about ecology, I think Christians could start by talking about the ecology of a marriage, the ecology of a family, the ecology of a neighbourhood. If we talk about the environment—the environment of the soul, the environment of the human heart—I think Christianity has a great deal to say. And then if the discussion of the environment goes beyond Christianity out into a wider circle, a wider world, a larger globe, so be it. We will take whatever truth comes in addition to what we have, but there are some unique gifts, there are some unique promises—prophecies, if you will—that come with the Christian tradition that are salvational now and later.

Alton: When I went to Liverpool as a student, we still had a sectarian party on the city council, which was still there when I was first elected to council, and it brought to mind that thirty years earlier the Catholic archbishop and the Anglican bishop would not even say the Lord's Prayer with one another because they didn't recognize each other's orders, and such was the relationship in a sectarian city. What a contrast when after the London bomb, standing on the steps of Liverpool Cathedral were the Anglican bishop, the Catholic archbishop, the local rabbi, the trustee of a local mosque, and the secretary of a Hindu cultural organization holding a sign that said "But not here". Now it seems to me this is the issue: how do we learn to live alongside one another respectfully? It is not quite saying, "Well, you were more concerned about idolatry than we were", or "We have all the answers to everything that confronts us"; it is not for those reasons at all. We enter into each other's lives, and we are enriched by that.

As a student, and I'll come back to the practical now, I spent two of my vacations thinking I was doing a bit of good because I taught immigrant children English. It did me more good than it probably did them. The children primarily came from Chinese backgrounds, they had come via Hong Kong, but many had escaped from Mao's China and the Cultural Revolution. Learning their stories was extraordinarily instructive for me. Hearing the suffering and the pain that they had gone through touched me. One of those families became very close friends of mine, and indeed one of the children of that family is my goddaughter. I mentioned her in a speech in Parliament this week in the House of Lords on Monday when I raised the issue of English as a Second Language. How can we have true integration in this country if we don't even give Syrian refugees and many others who are here living in this country the opportunity to learn our language? ESL courses have been cut by 60 per cent over the last ten years. This is a crazy thing to do. It touches on something very fundamental—that is, our identity. I do not need to surrender my identity to enter into other people's lives. Isaiah said, "Consider the rock from which you were hewn" (Isaiah 51:1, New Jerusalem Bible), and wasn't it King Croesus of the Lydians who went to the oracle and asked, "What is the most important thing a man should know?" And the oracle replied, "Know who you are". Know who you are. So I am a Christian, but that does not stop me recognizing the gifts that other people bring to the table and learning to live alongside them is crucially important. Next month in December we will commemorate the seventieth anniversary of two things. One is the genocide convention. Hold that in mind when you think about what happened to Yazidis, Christians, Shia Muslims, Jews, Shabaks, Mandeans, and other minorities in northern Iraq and Syria. The other anniversary is the universal declaration of human rights. Article 18 says, "Everyone shall have the right to believe, not to believe, or to change their belief." It's honoured in the breach all over the world. This is something that brings us together. One million Uighurs were sent to re-education camps in China. Rohingya Muslims were persecuted alongside Christians in Burma. Raif Badawi was humiliated and beaten in Saudi Arabia because he was an atheist, and Alexander Aan spent four years in prison in Indonesia because he posted on his Facebook profile that he didn't believe in God. We have to stand alongside one another, stop measuring how much we believe in something against how much someone else believes in something, and stop trying to set up mutual rivalries that will take us nowhere.

Comment by Geoff O'Donoghue
Good evening and thank you very much. This is partially a question, but maybe more an observation prompted by the question about where we find this empathic capacity that will be required in our modern world. All this talk about the self prompted me to reflect on what Pope Francis said about the sacred and reconnecting with the sacred in our lives and in our world. And he spoke about that very explicitly in terms of understanding the sacred in all things, the interconnectedness of all things. But he also made it very clear that this was an ancient knowledge; it was not a new knowledge that was being imparted. For myself, if I go back in my own ancestors, Celtic ancestors, when they sat down to milk a cow, they put their hand on the side of the cow. In that very moment, they gave thanks for the bounty of that moment and for the gift that they were about to receive, and it was that close—their understanding of the sacred, the sacred nature of God and of all things, and the sacred nature of themselves and the animal that they were encountering was all part of a single relationship. And I think this is the call that we have been given again, because of the degree to which we are individually able to reconnect with what is sacred: with our God,

however we express that; with the sacred in the person; and with the sacred in every creature. When this happens on the earth, it seems to me that it will prompt service, and it will be the kind of service that heals and is what is needed for this next stage.

Holland: That probably wasn't a question; it was a major message. That was wonderful. But inherent in that comment, it seems to me, is the reminder that life is noisy, things are busy, there are distractions; there are competing urgencies and demands. As I mentioned earlier in my brief remarks, even the living Son of the living God had to get away, had to retreat, go into the mountains, get away from the crowd even though he was committed to the crowd and all the purposes and all the needs of that crowd. I think you have given a wonderful statement about the constant need to renew, to look inside, to reflect, to meditate and respond and pray. Only then can we be fortified to re-engage and come back for the battle. But we need to remember that at some point that tank of fuel can run out. We need to renew, we need to refortify, until it is there, the holiness is there, the sanctity is there. I believe that if we take the time to get away from the noise, move away from motion, we are better prepared to engage in the substance of what this conversation has been about here tonight.

Williams: I am very glad that you have foregrounded this idea of the sacred because it seems to me that to acknowledge the sacred is to recognize there is something that we absolutely and fundamentally do not own. And the idea that we own, have a right over, or possess something, whether it is the world we are in or another person, is the absolute opposite of anything we could understand as service. So my question, really, is for all of us and for our culture: what are the processes and habits we educate our people in, especially children and young people? Do we give them the opportunity to experience the world as something that is not owned? Other people as realities that are not owned? How do we get that pause, that hesitation, that distance that allows us to see that this is not us, this is not our property? That can be in all sorts of ways, and I do wonder whether our education system at every level really gives those opportunities to young people with the more functionalist, busy, and anxious we get as educators. That's another story that is with us.

Teal: Geoff O'Donoghue is international director of CAFOD (the Catholic Fund for Overseas Development), and I think he is able to answer any questions tonight if anyone is interested in spending time with that organization. Thank you so very much to everybody who is here tonight, because it has been an experience of people really wanting to engage and question, and it's been like watching something alive and kaleidoscopic—changing with illumination and colour from different directions, so we have witnessed texture, nuance, and integrity. I do not think I am alone in being absolutely delighted that this evening has gone the way it has and in being profoundly thankful to our speakers.

Notes

[1] C. S. Lewis, "Vivisection", in *C. S. Lewis: Essay Collection and Other Short Pieces* (London: Fount, Harper Collins, 2000), pp. 693–97.

[2] See Richard Higgins, "Thoreau and Trees: A Visceral Connection", 2 June 2016, <https://www.americanforests.org/magazine/article/thoreau-trees-a-visceral-connection/>, accessed 14 August 2020.

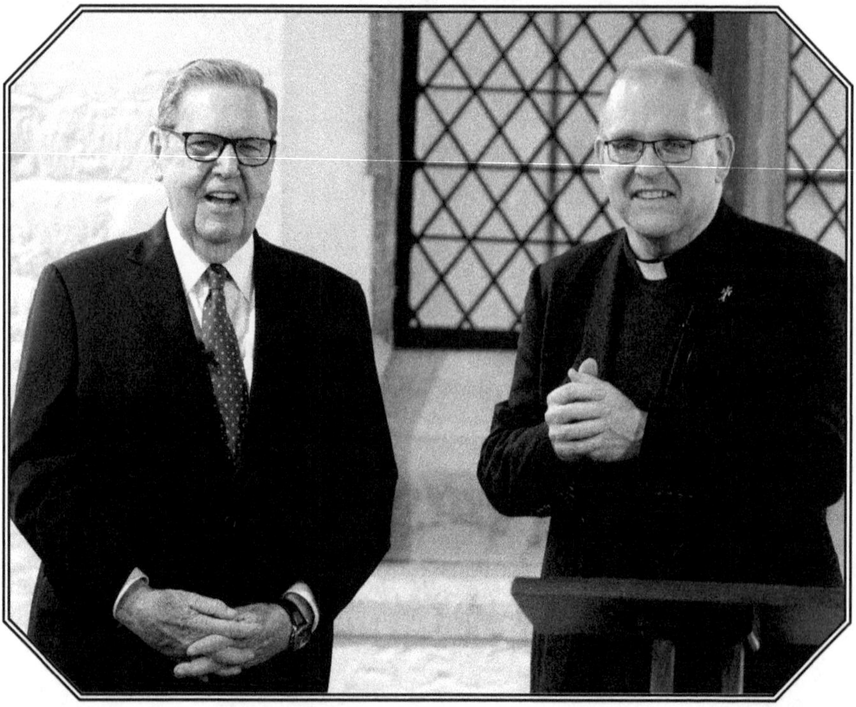

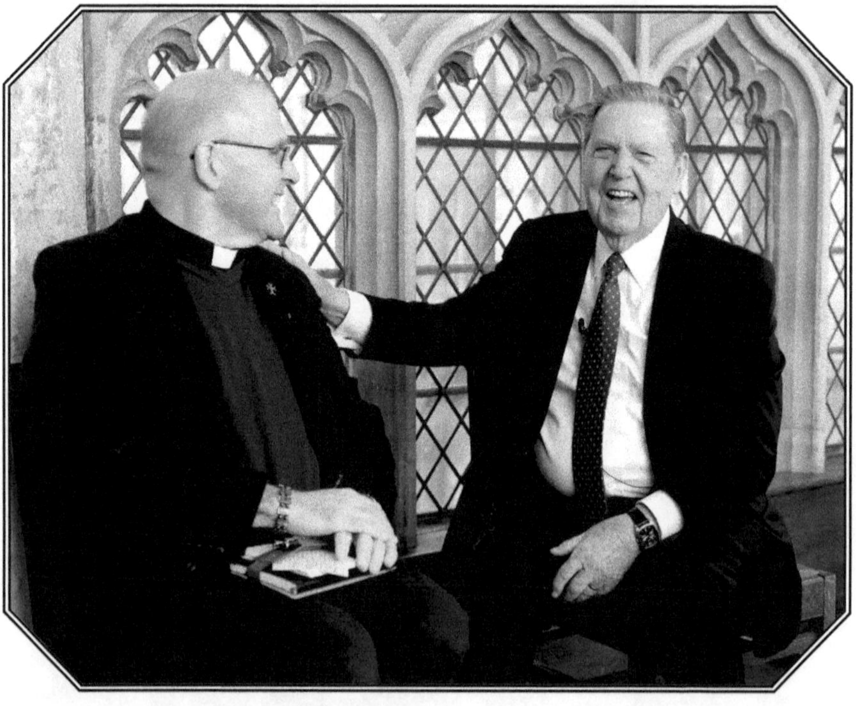

2

The Restored Gospel

Jeffrey R. Holland with Andrew Teal

The following remarks and question and answer session took place at the University Church of St Mary the Virgin, Oxford, under the auspices of the University of Oxford's Faculty of Theology and Religion on 22 November 2018.

Holland: Thank you, Professor Paul Kerry; we acknowledge your role here at the university and the wonderful relationships you've built and the kindness of the Reverend Doctor Andrew Teal, whom we love and admire as a friend. We are grateful for the hospitality that we feel here today.

Andrew has invited me to speak for a few minutes about The Church of Jesus Christ of Latter-day Saints, its doctrine and practice, and then allow some question and answer time. I want to say at the outset that I am anxiously trying not to be off-balance here. I realize I am over from the colonies, so that in itself is a little unsettling. The other unsettling thing is that although I know my own theological vocabulary, I nevertheless want to make sure that I honour the language Andrew will use. That leads me to the only humour I will be able to work into this talk, and I hope it is humorous. When doing background work for this lecture, I discovered that the very earliest Anglo-Saxons did not have a concept of eternity. It was then I realized that was how the game of cricket was created. [laughter] If I fall back or fall short, please understand at the outset that I love this country. I have lived here for more than five years of my life and am proud to be the true anglophile in our quorum and in our Church leadership.

71

I'm anxious to share information with you today that will be more substantial than the clichéd humour that somehow still manages to find its way around regarding polygamy, which we do not practise, or the fact that there are double decker buses this very hour circling Piccadilly Circus and the neighbouring Theatre District in London, pleading for everyone to see *The Book of Mormon* musical. In contradiction to those buses and those billboards, we would prefer that people read the Book of Mormon rather than see the show, but I suppose we will just let that go as show business does. If all that you know about The Church of Jesus Christ of Latter-day Saints is what you glean from pop culture or street conversation, you probably do neither yourselves nor us the adequate justice that I hope I can summon today.

We believe that we are coming to you and to the world in fulfilment of an ancient prophecy from the gifted prophet Isaiah:

> Be drunk, but not from wine; stagger, but not from strong drink! For the Lord has poured out upon you a spirit of deep sleep; he has closed your eyes, you prophets, and covered your heads, you seers.... So I will again do amazing things with this people, shocking and amazing. The wisdom of their wise shall perish, and the discernment of the discerning shall be hidden.... And those who err in spirit will come to understanding, and those who grumble will accept instruction.
>
> Isaiah 29:9–10,14,24

In coming to know us, you'll learn quickly that we believe not only in God the Eternal Father, His Son Jesus Christ, and the Holy Ghost but also in angels—resurrected beings, divine messages, and messengers of all scriptural kinds. In a word, we believe in modern revelation as it was given in past dispensations and which we believe should always characterize the true Church of God.

That is an essential prelude to my message because we believe the dawn of that marvellous work and wonder, to which Isaiah referred, came in the spring of 1820 when a young man not yet fifteen years of age desired to know if the true, original New Testament Church of Jesus Christ was still on the earth. Acting on pure faith and in response to a single biblical verse, James 1:5, "If any of you is lacking in wisdom, ask God, who gives to all generously and ungrudgingly, and it will be given you", that boy, with the plainest of Anglo-Saxon names, Joseph Smith Jr., prayed vocally for the first time in his life. In response to that prayer, what happened next is, to believers like myself, the most important revelatory event for mortals to have witnessed or to have heard about since that little band of disciples gathered on the Mount of Olives to witness Christ's final hours on earth. On that day of ascension, two angels had said to the group, "Men of Galilee, why do you stand looking up towards heaven? This Jesus, who has been taken up from you into heaven, will come in the same way as you saw him go into heaven" (Acts 1:11). Just days later, the Apostle Peter added, "[He] who must remain in heaven until the time of universal restoration that God announced long ago through his holy prophets" (Acts 3:21). We believe that spring day in 1820 was the beginning of that second messianic return in a vision, which the young Joseph Smith described as being "above the brightness of the sun" (Joseph Smith—History 1:16). God the Eternal Father and his resurrected Son, Jesus Christ, appeared to him in breathtaking glory.

This is our message to the world—and surely you have seen some of our approximately seventy thousand young missionaries that are labouring around the world sharing that message—that the day of restitution prophesied so long ago has begun, including a step-by-step restoration of all that was in the primitive Church, including twelve Apostles and the other Church offices of that day—all in anticipation of Christ's triumphant, much more public and final, return to rule and reign as King of kings. The appearance to young Joseph Smith was only the precursor. So the day of that vision in 1820 is inextricably linked with my day at Oxford with you.

Both days presuppose certain truths. One of those is that in New Testament times there was a true Church, of which Jesus Christ was the chief cornerstone and the personification of divinity, with mortal men called as prophets and apostles to form a foundational structure around him. These Apostles with other teachers and priests, pastors and members, constituted a figurative building—a Church, if you will—fitly framed together, which Paul described as "to equip the saints for the work of ministry, for building up the body of Christ" (Ephesians 4:12).

Another truth fundamental to my visit with you today is that the New Testament Church was expected to exist, or at least it is assumed it was expected to continue to exist, until that glorious, final appearance of which these angels spoke of in the book of Acts. There were Jesus's teachings to be taught, his saving ordinances and sacraments to be embraced, and a community of believers to be established that would serve and strengthen individuals, families, neighbourhoods, and nations by putting on what Paul called "the whole armour of God" (Ephesians 6:11).

Sadly, however, the Church did not withstand what Paul went on to call "the wiles of the devil" and "the cosmic powers of this present darkness" (Ephesians 6:11–12). After Christ's ascension and the gradual, inexorable death of the early Apostles, the divinity of the Church and its orderly succession of ordained, authorized priesthood administers was gradually lost, removed from the human family. Without apostolic keys and authorized priestly oversight, over time the doctrine either eroded or in some cases was corrupted, and unauthorized changes to the saving ordinances were introduced. What then ensued was more than a millennium of institutional darkness, leading to the divisions and divergence and religious disarray of many kinds and dashing Paul's hopes that there would be a unity of the faith and a knowledge of the Son of God. It belabours the obvious to note that in the Christian world we do not enjoy anything remotely approximating a unity of faith today, nor a common church fitly framed together. Indeed, those in the contemporary religious culture—if we can call it that—particularly the young, seem well and truly "tossed to and fro, and blown about by every wind of doctrine" (Ephesians 4:14). But Paul still gives voice to all who would yearn for that "one Lord, one faith, one baptism" (Ephesians 4:5) of the original New Testament Church.

And so it was in Joseph Smith's day; the young boy prophet lamented that his region was a scene of great confusion and bad feeling: priest contending against priest, convert against convert so that any good feelings were entirely lost in a "war of words and a tumult of opinions" (Joseph Smith—History 1:10). That confusion led to the prayer I have mentioned and the theophany that followed. So, what brings me to you today is not a message of reformation but of restoration. The Church that Christ established by his hand in the meridian of time has been restored by his own hand in this present time. This is a fundamental way in which The Church of Jesus Christ of Latter-day Saints is for the most part distinct from most, virtually all, of contemporary Christian churches—a distinction without which one cannot fully understand our history, our doctrine, or our fervour in sending out missionaries to all the world. Our basic message, then, about Christ's restored Church and doctrine is not limited to but might begin with these truths.

First, every man, woman, and child who has ever lived, now lives, or will yet live, so long as the earth shall last, is a son or daughter of a loving and divine Heavenly Father. He is the God in whose image we were created as the spiritual offspring to God. We are "heirs of God and joint-heirs with Christ" (Romans 8:17). To gain a mortal body and experience moral growth available in no other way, a real Adam and a real Eve chose to leave the paradisiacal setting—Eden, if you will—to learn all that was necessary for the children of God to learn. They especially learned about living together in love and realized that the guidance of God would give them the only real answers to personal and familial, social and political, economic and philosophical problems that they would face in mortality. Because mistakes would be made in the course of the mortal education, sometimes horrible mistakes, a Saviour was provided for such a plan, one that would not only atone for Adam and Eve's initial transgression but also for every individual transgression that was made for all those in the human family: the sins and sorrows, the disappointments and despair, the tears and tragedy of every man, woman, and child who would ever live. Such a plan was necessary, and such a Saviour was required because life is eternal. Our hopes and dreams mattered before we came to this earth, and they will most certainly matter after we leave it. We say with Job, "After my skin has been thus destroyed, then in my flesh I shall see God" (Job 19:26), and say with the Apostle Paul, "If for this life only we have hoped in Christ, we are of all people most to be pitied" (1 Corinthians 15:19). Lastly, this plan, this divine course outlined for us, including the fortunate Fall in Eden and the redemption of Gethsemane and Calvary, is universally inclusive. All are children of the same God, and all are included in his love and his grace. "For as all die in Adam, so all will be made alive in Christ" (1 Corinthians 15:22). Everyone is covered, though it remains to be seen whether everyone cares, but if there is a failure to respond it won't be because God didn't try and Christ didn't come. That is at the heart of what I have been introducing to you as the restored gospel.

Now in light of what I considered is reasonably straightforward biblical theology, one may wonder: Why did these Latter-day Saints stir up such emotions in people, and why are they not considered Christian by some? Let me conclude with just a few thoughts on that. We are not considered Christian by some because we are not fourth-century Christians; we are not Nicaean Christians; we are not creedal Christians of the brand that arose hundreds of years after Christ. No, when we speak of restored Christianity, we speak of the Church as it was in its New Testament time, not as it became when great councils were called to debate and anguish over what it was that they really believed. So if one means Greek-influenced, council-convening, philosophy-flavoured Christianity opposed to Christianity in apostolic times, we are not generally considered that kind of Christian. Thus, we teach that God the Father and his Son Jesus Christ are separate and distinct beings with glorified bodies of flesh and bone. As such we stand with the historical position that the formal doctrine of the Trinity as it was defined by the great Church councils of the fourth and fifth centuries is not to be found in the New Testament.

We take Christ literally at his word that he came down from heaven not to do his will but the will of him who sent him. Of his antagonists, he said they have "hated both me and my Father" (John 15:24).These along with scores of other references, including his pleading prayers, make clear Jesus's physical separation from his Father. However, having affirmed the point of their separate and distinct physical nature, we declare unequivocally that they are indeed one in every other conceivable way—in mind, in deed, in will, in wish, in hope, in faith, in purpose, in intent, and in love, but they are separate and distinct individuals as fathers and sons are. In this matter, we differ from traditional creedal Christianity but do agree with the New Testament perception.

We also differ from fourth- and fifth-century Christianity by declaring that the scriptural canon is not closed, that the heavens are open with revelatory experience, and that God meant what he said when he promised Moses, "My works are without end, and also my words, for they never cease" (Moses 1:4). The Book of Mormon, which is subtitled

"Another Testament of Jesus Christ", and other canonized scripture as well as the role of living oracles bear witness to the fact that God continues to speak and to guide his children here on earth. Coupled with the Holy Bible, there is no document more powerful than the Book of Mormon as evidence of God's continuing, loving voice and as witness of the divinity of the Lord Jesus Christ. The Book of Mormon is that other half of Isaiah's prophecy with which we began, of which the prophet went on to say, "The vision of all this has become for you like the words of a sealed document. On that day the deaf shall hear the words of a scroll, and out of their gloom and darkness the eyes of the blind shall see. The meek shall obtain fresh joy in the LORD, and the neediest people shall exult in the Holy One of Israel" (Isaiah 29:11,18–19). I, for one, would feel to walk on hot lava and chew broken glass if I could find a document, any document anywhere, containing any new words of Christ—fifty words, twenty words, one new word from the Son of God—let alone hundreds of pages that record the appearance, teachings, covenants, and counsel he gave to a heretofore unknown audience. Because I want you neither to walk on hot lava nor chew broken glass, I have gifted copies of the Book of Mormon for those of you that would like one at the end of this lecture.

In any case we agree enthusiastically with the insightful Protestant scholar who inquired, "On what biblical or historical grounds has the inspiration of God been limited to the written documents that the church now calls its Bible? . . . If the Spirit inspired only the written documents of the first century, does that mean that the same Spirit does not speak today about matters that are of significant concern?"[1] Lastly, for today, we're unique in the modern Christian world regarding another matter, which a prophet and a president of The Church of Jesus Christ of Latter-day Saints called our most distinguishing characteristic, that is divine priesthood authority to provide the living sacraments, the saving sacraments, the ordinances of the gospel of Jesus Christ. The holy priesthood, which has been restored to the earth by those who held it anciently, signals the return of divine authorization. It is different from all other man-made powers and authorities on the face of the earth. Without it there could be a church in name only, and it would be a church lacking in authority to administer the things of God. This restoration of priesthood authority eases centuries of anguish among those who knew certain ordinances and sacraments were essential, but lived with the doubt as to who had the right to administer them.

Breaking ecclesiastically with his more famous brother John over the latter's decision to ordain without any divine authority to do so, Charles Wesley wrote:

> How easily are bishops made
> By man or woman's whim:
> Wesley his hands on Coke hath laid,
> But who laid hands on him?[2]

In The Church of Jesus Christ of Latter-day Saints, we can answer the question of who laid hands on him all the way back to Christ himself. The return of such authority is truly the most distinguishing feature of our faith. Not long ago I happened across a quotation from one who had a ministry, not in England but in New England, a century ago. This plain-spoken cleric wrote:

> The loss of respect for religion is the dry rot of social institutions. The idea of God as the Creator and Father of all mankind is to the moral world, what gravitation is in the natural; it holds everything else together and causes it to revolve around a common center. Take away that and any ultimate significance to life falls apart. There is then no such thing as collective humanity, but only separate molecules of men and women drifting in the universe with no more cohesion and no more meaning than so many grains of sand have meaning for the sea.[3]

I hope I've said something that can counter the loss of respect for religion and expunge what in some settings is the dry rot of modern, social institutions. My convictions about The Church of Jesus Christ of Latter-day Saints and the gospel of Jesus Christ mean everything to me. Certainly it is the common centre of my existence around which everything else revolves. It produces, protects, promises, or points to every good thing I possess now or hope to possess in the future. Thank you for your attendance; I am honoured by your invitation and complimented by courtesy and hospitality. I say that expressly of my beloved friend Andrew Teal. May the love of God be with us all and may the Church, the truth of Christ, and the truth in Christ save our souls and make us free. In the name of Jesus Christ, amen. Andrew, thank you.

Teal: Thank you, Elder Holland. It is great to be here in this historic place that Elder Holland was commenting on. On this Thanksgiving Day, it is great to be here together. There was another theological conversation in the sixteenth century between Thomas Cranmer and some persecutors, and so I hope that the outcome of today's gathering will be a lot better for all of us. But Broad Street is just right there for whatever. [laughter]

Holland: Is that smoke I can smell? [laughter]

Teal: This is also a place where the Oxford Movement began, which transformed and challenged the nature of the Church of England to ask deep questions about, among other things, apostolic succession. And it's where a former vicar of this church, John Henry Newman, came to terms with the fact that apostolic succession was one of the things that could not be argued back into the nature of the Church of England. Apostolic succession seemed to be a real hot potato. This is also the very room where Oxfam was founded in 1942, so it's a great thing on this Thanksgiving Day. There are a lot of things to be grateful for and most particularly Elder Holland. It's a long path from Salt Lake City, but the path of Christianity is even longer. It's a moving path, where only God is both consistent and true, and he has integrity as he moves with us through the steps of time. With his support we find new words and renewed life to bear witness to journey with real tensions. We want to be consistent with what is true and what has been revealed, and we also want to say that actually, for us, the golden age is not in the past; archaeology is not the answer; it's eschatology; it's the end-time. On this path there have been many stages of development and change. My specific research area is the fourth and fifth centuries, and one of the things that you find there is that people like Athanasius will use words, different words, in order to try to move things on, and now even those ways of seeing things can be recognized as important even if we later look to other emphases in doctrine.[4] Steps the Christian community had to take as a sort of progression, in time, may have to be reviewed again. An Anglican theologian, Richard Hooker, said (and I paraphrase!), "That which was once best might now be worst."[5] He wanted to say that in early Anglicanism there needs to be a real determination to bear witness of the significance of this journey and Christ, the one who accompanies us—he is the one who teaches, mentors, eats with, and travels with us, coming bearing eternal truths. Our theological conjectures tell us more about ourselves than him all too often, but his patience is astounding!

Today we can listen together and commit to a real determination to discuss, a commitment to really understand, to explore, to enjoy, and to converse with true love and affection. This commitment is almost radiantly palpable, and that doesn't mean we need to collapse into politeness—far from it. Respect and love allow a real openness to truth. Therefore, I think all of us here, I hope, are determined to be aware that our history should not collapse our discussion today into distant categories so that we can label one another.

For example, one of the things that I have been discussing with Paul Kerry is the nature of language describing the personhood of God. God isn't like Wi-Fi, which is here interfering with our mobile phones and making strange noises, but God always comes in a personal way. He always comes incarnate and rather than say, "Well, when you talk about the personhood of God and the embodiment of God, that's the anthropomorphite controversy of whatever century" we are obliged to ask ourselves: What is the language of the tripersonal God and his unity? Can we commit to working together and finding a vision of the God who weeps at human brokenness, lack of hospitality, and harshness of mind and heart, yet who doesn't abandon us but time after time draws near?

So that's what I really hope is the beginning of a significant journey to say we need to understand each other and work together and love one another.

I suppose the first question is a really steep path. There is no rehearsal for this. A friend of mine gave me a small sign to put on the door that said "You're never ready for what you have to do: you just do it. That makes you ready." And we, as humans, don't like that. We like to have everything carefully prepared and secure, especially if we are involved in organizing things like this. So the question is: On this journey, how does The Church of Jesus Christ of Latter-day Saints try to form people into a consistently flexible community? What's been difficult in helping people to take some things as eternally true and to see that it is likely that other things will change? I know all of our churches have changed massively, but that doesn't exclude some very significant challenges that we must face together. What is that formation like?

Holland: I think, Andrew, probably a fundamental principle for us in this regard would be the principle of ongoing revelation. It reinforces the fact that we need to be tentative to some degree when looking back and looking forward. We realize that God has not revealed everything that he is going to reveal. One of our articles of faith is that we believe that God has revealed, does now reveal, and will yet reveal great saving truths, and that has an impact on us individually and as an institution. It has an impact on individual faith and belief, so I think it's obligatory for us to remain open (perhaps tentative is not as good a word as open) to reflection, review, history, insight, and revelatory experience. Whether that is in scientific, economic, political, or more straightforward theological terms, we need to be open to that. We can't be fixed; we, by definition, can't be locked into a position that is not open to continuing revelation. Whether we honour that well can be a matter of opinion. Some of us are more rigid than others, but I think that would not be the fault of the Church. The Church is solidly predicated on the idea of revelation.

Teal: The central question that I think Jesus asks is always "Who do you say that I am?" (Matthew 16:15), and that's quite a hard question to answer, but today we have heard about his relation to God the Father, and his distinctness from God the Father. So already we are in the realms of mystery and revealed mercy. Frederick William Faber, one of Newman's friends, said, "There's a wideness in God's mercy, like the wideness of the sea. There's a kindness in God's justice, which is more than liberty."[6] And I think that connects with what you said about how, in fact, part of the gospel committed to us is revealing a God that is more generous in his views and boundless in his mercy and blessings than we can conceive. So does the genre of doctrine have to be honed to what you described as the eternal gospel, that there is no one who ever has been or ever will be, who can't be a part of that wonderful blessing? Is that the defining boundary?

Holland: If I understand the question, you are probing a basic, defining principle for us. Salvation, as extended through the plan of God and the incarnation, the ministry, and the Atonement of his Son, is all-inclusive. Every man, woman, and child ever to exist is covered by the atoning grace and mercy of Jesus Christ. Because of this gift, there are some things that are expected in terms of a godly walk; there are some implications of this belief that would dictate how people should behave. We do believe firmly in the sacraments; we do believe in ordinances, but we believe those come as a consequence of one's faith and as a response to the feelings that he or she has had in coming to understand the universal gift of Christ's Atonement. Down through the centuries, in the era of the Old Testament, people would have known a great deal about God's justice, they would have known a great deal about his omnipotence, they would have known a great deal, on occasion, about his anger, but I think what he had not been able to convey successfully to us as mortals was his love and his mercy. So the ultimate gift and manifestation of who God is was the embodiment and the incarnation of his Son. It was through the life of Christ, God's greatest gift and his greatest blessing, that the Father primarily showed the grace, mercy, and love that we know of, teach of, testify of, and identify with. That brings us back full circle to the idea of God and Christ's unity, for their mercy, truth, grace, and love is the same. The only distinction between them that we make is that they were and are two physically distinct beings, that when Christ prayed, he was praying to someone. When he said, "Father, forgive them" (Luke 23:34), he was talking to his Father and asking for forgiveness to be extended to his tormentors. But other than that physical distinction, the unity, especially of their love, mercy, and grace, is inseparable, inextricable—a witness that we're anxious to bear and have understood as our institutional position.

Teal: One of the things I think that other churches, other denominations, find puzzling is the baptism for the dead, which the Apostle Paul writes about, but you've viewed this as an extension of the mission of mercy.

Holland: That's exactly right.

Teal: In the Orthodox tradition of the twentieth century, a great, saintly man named Silouan the Athonite experienced the devastation of the Bolshevik Revolution on the Orthodox Christian community. For him, too, it was heartbreaking to see the destruction and desecration of cathedrals and churches and the fabric of faithfulness. Another Russian visited him on Mount Athos. He said, "'God will punish all atheists. They will burn in everlasting fire.' Obviously upset, the Staretz said, 'Tell me, supposing you went to paradise, and there looked down and saw somebody burning in hellfire—would you feel happy?' 'It can't be helped. It would be their own fault,' said the hermit. [Silouan] answered him with a sorrowful countenance: 'Love could not bear that,' he said, 'we must pray for *all*.'"[7] In this city, and very probably in this very location, the Anglican Church rediscovered the nature of the *infinite* Atonement and a Christian responsibility to pray for others, the living and the dead, in the name and authority of Him who lived and died and who grasped all in every kind of self-alienation and despair, the living and the dead. We trust that those prayers will gently lead all to Jesus Christ with devotion, care, humility, self-sacrifice, and compassion. So the extension of an actual sacrament to the dead in some churches is the Absolution of the Dead. In a way, is this a manner of understanding baptism for the dead?

Holland: Indeed, it is. For us it would be a cosmic, monumental injustice to say that someone who had never even heard the name Jesus Christ and was born in an era where that language wasn't used and in a culture where it was not understood would be condemned to hell, that somehow these people could be cast off through no act or choice of their own. To pass judgement because of the inadvertence of their birth and ancestry would seem to be the most blatant injustice of eternity. So, as you noted, Andrew, we do perform a vicarious ordinance, as Paul taught, but its acceptance is optional. I don't know whether there are attorneys in the room, but the vicarious ordinances performed are an "offer" to the dead, and of course offers have to be accepted to be contractually binding. We are not assuming that everybody is going to accept that ordinance or that they will choose Christ any more there than they chose him here in mortality. But we do believe that it would be a terrible injustice and no act of mercy in any way to preclude people simply because they were born in a time, place, era, culture, or dispensation where the gospel of Jesus Christ was not available or his name was not even known. To provide for them is a part of that universal embrace that we speak of.

Teal: There are many people who live inspiring lives and can bring about a reorientation towards God in every generation. Can you envisage a day when, through conversation, common understanding, and prayer, Joseph Smith will be recognized as a prophet for the broader Christian Church? Can you envisage a day when people will say, "Lay aside some of the aggression and recognize that he was a human being in his era—a simple, ordinary man to whom the living God spoke, and through whom he worked," and would that be something that you would hope for?

Holland: Oh, I would definitely hope for that! Whether I can envision it or not, I'm not sure, but I can hope for it. I would hope for it on the basis of merit. To use Joseph Smith as the example, I would hope for it on the basis of what he taught, seeing that as consistent with what seems true, what sounds true, what feels true, and is consistent with what you, or I, believe is true. So I wouldn't expect such loyalty in the absence of faith. I wouldn't ask that someone suspend reason and good judgement and accept my witness just because I say it, but I would invite the kind of investigation that asks: What did Joseph Smith teach? What did he stand for? I would ask the same of someone investigating Peter, Paul, or anyone else of such standing, and let the truth fall where it may, let that spiritual conviction come if it comes. That is one of the reasons why I believe that one of the first gifts, one of the first of the Church's institutional messages to the world came in the form of the book. It was tangible; it was readable; it was shareable; it was portable. And it didn't rely on an act of faith, though faith is ultimately at the basis of everything one believes. The Book of Mormon doesn't require blind faith. It was intended to start an open conversation, then let the merit of the conversation carry the reader where it will. That kind of universality for The Church of Jesus Christ of Latter-day Saints I can envision, and it's what I would truly hope for. Then I would let the truth and spiritual witnesses come where they come, taking our chances with that.

Teal: One question that is interesting is that some other early Christians speculate that there were two creations, a spiritual one and then the Fall, and the Fall is why we are in flesh. Now that seems to be rather different from what you were saying about how, in fact, there is a premortal existence of men and women, and the Fall is not so much a fall but a step, a pedagogical, educational step. So does that mean that the Fall of Adam and Eve was a choice?

Holland: We are fairly emphatic about the reality of Adam and Eve and impact of the Fall. We do talk about the Fall and about a fallen world as part of a plan linked to the Atonement of Jesus Christ. We do not see it as an ignorant step. We believe that the exit from the Garden of Eden was given as an option and that Adam and Eve could have theoretically stayed in the garden forever. But it is also our doctrine that if they had chosen to stay in the garden, then none of the rest of us could have joined them on earth. So, they chose to leave in order that we might be. They chose with the understanding that there would be a Saviour who would come and be, as Paul said in Corinthians, another "Adam" (1 Corinthians 15:45,47). And so Adam and Eve were involved in the Fall, and the other Adam, Christ, was involved in the redemption. And so you get that little couplet, "For as all die in Adam, so all will be made alive in Christ" (1 Corinthians 15:22). They become the bookends of a plan that brings us into mortality, gives us learning and a physical body, then provides a way for us to leave with a resurrected body, which we all celebrate, and which, I think, is sometimes too understated in Christianity. When we talk about an unembodied God, it's hard for me to reconcile that with all the emphasis that Christians supposedly place on the Resurrection. What was so significant about the Resurrection if we don't see a need for divinity to be embodied? Yes, we are very emphatic about the Fall, but it was a fortunate fall; it was a step, knowingly made, into mortality with some promises conveyed that would reassure Adam and Eve that there was a way up out of that Fall, into eternal life.

Teal: There is an ancient hymn of the earliest Church called the *Exsultet* sung during the night of Easter, and one of the couplets from that is "O happy fault, O necessary sin of Adam".[8]

Holland: That could be our hymn; we could adopt that.

Teal: I will send you a copy! But it seems to be a celebration of our bodies; it gives the sense of a happy fall that is the foundation of the Resurrection. And this thing about bodies, enjoying looking after and engaging with our bodies, seems to be in the culture of The Church of Jesus Christ of Latter-day Saints. For example, there appears to be a real enjoyment of things like dancing. In fact, if I could quote a Latter-day Saint singer of a group called The Killers, Brandon Flowers, there is a song with lyrics "Are we human or are we dancer?", and I actually think the answer is that we are both.

Holland: Both. We haven't gone around as advance men for The Killers, but we acknowledge that truth in their song.

Teal: But the *Exsultet* is better then?

Holland: Right, and so is the Tabernacle Choir!

Questions and Responses

Question 1

I have the first question. When you spoke, you mentioned a time of overt persecution of the Church and that we must strive for something like normalization or the idea of overcoming the distance we put between ourselves. Could you explain and expand on that? What are your thoughts?

Teal: I remember Elder Holland saying how the Latter-day Saint community brings with them the experience of being the only community, as far as I am aware, in the United States that had an order for extermination.

Holland: That's right, an extermination order.

Teal: That was in Independence, Missouri. But in a sense, that prompted, despite it being a dreadful thing, a journey and, if you like, the carving of a frontier spirituality.

Holland: It played a significant part in forming the character of the Church in its first century of existence.

Teal: With progression there also comes opposition, aggressive reactions, and attempts to undermine.

Holland: I think that tension will always exist. For us, it had a very binding, covenantal impact. It drew those pioneers, those refugees, together. They depended on each other very, very much; thus was born an early heritage of service, care, and watching out for each other. But, Andrew, I also think the idea is important that although we were even driven, quite literally, across the United States and finally beyond the then existing territorial lines of the United States, we never felt like we were retreating from or taking ourselves outside of that community. Almost immediately after arriving in the Great Basin, there was a spirit of growth, education, and engagement in the political processes that would allow us to return to the community. We've never seen ourselves as being a community that wanted to be "loners", to be outside the circle of a Christian, cultural, or political community. I think the history of the Church now shows that return. A year or two ago, we had not one but two candidates running for president of the United States who were members of The Church of Jesus Christ of Latter-day Saints. For me, I wouldn't have cared very much for the negative political consequences that surely would have come to the Church had either won, but the symbol of these candidates running shows that we meant to return, planned to return, and have returned to be part of the larger community and be in a normalized, comfortable relationship with our neighbour. We have worked very hard at that and have tried to make sure that we are inclusive and not exclusive.

Question 2

We live in a time when many social justice advocates are saying that religion is out of touch, that it fails to meet the needs of large groups of constituents including women, the LGBTQ+ community, minorities, and individuals. However, a theology student of deity and Christian theology, and specifically of The Church of Jesus Christ of Latter-day Saints, will find answers to many of these claims. Attention is being brought to lost scriptures that exonerate women and an existence of a divine Heavenly Mother alongside the Father. However, these doctrines remain largely trapped in theological discussions, out of reach of the average religious discourse. Therefore, how can we bring these great theological truths, which for too long have been regarded as deeper theology, to the surface level in order to answer these claims that the Church is no longer in touch with common humanity?

Holland: That's a great question; that's a great speech. Did we get that all down? I actually think what Andrew Teal is doing this very minute with us and what he does with others, such as with my two sons and Paul Kerry, is to encourage that kind of conversation. I've heard him use the word conversation a dozen times since we met on the street and walked up here, and that is a compliment to Andrew. It shows that he really wants that climate, that attitude, that openness: the openness of both personal and institutional faith. We are not always this welcomed; we are not always so warmly invited, in many places. So there are symbolic steps in understanding, like this very experience today and the freedom you have to ask that very question. We need to find ways to do more of this. When we have these conversations, what we'll find is that we have far more in common than we have differences. In unity we will have more impact, more energy, and far more inspiration. We've let some differences, and I acknowledge that there are significant doctrinal distinctions, get in the way of warmer, wonderful conversations wherein we realize we have much in common and that much good can be done together. Earlier, I referred to the declining respect for religion being termed the "dry rot of social institutions". We must never allow religion to be relegated to the position of some sort of ancient appendix that is essentially useless, can be dangerous, and needs to be excised for safety's sake. Religion is still the answer to the world's problems. A little nun, when they discovered her effects, had just a sari or two, a sweater, and a little three-by-five card by her scriptures that said "With God all the rules are fair, and there are wonderful surprises". We need to engage in the surprising part; we need to start to talk about those, because surprises are available right now. We just need to talk about them more.

Teal: One of the things that I think is wonderfully clear is that there is a lack of defensiveness in this conversation. And if you read some of the things that are produced by The Church of Jesus Christ of Latter-day Saints, there is a recognition of much common ground. I remember hearing somebody say, "It may be a million miles away from where I am, but whatever you are, wherever you've been, come and talk, and we will try to be clean together. We will try to respect one another and build each other up." And there's that sense of recognition, respect, and dignity.

This means openness. We represent institutions, which are important, and we have to recognize that there are times when we have been a million miles away from embrace, understanding, and the twinkling of an eye when we disagree with something. We can still smile and be friends and keep on working on misunderstandings and disagreement. And that works in terms of doctrine, but it also works in terms of how all the mainstream religions, not just Christianity, have treated women, how they've treated people of different classes, how they've prioritized some people. All of that needs to be owned and addressed.

Holland: And the first obligation forever and ever is that we love God and love each other. If we could remember that, begin with that, and do that, I can't really imagine a serious conversation getting into trouble. Sometimes we leap to other issues and other differences, including doctrinal differences, and forget, unfortunately, that we're committed to love. If we can just anchor ourselves there, then I think we'll find an answer to other questions that we have.

Question 3

I love this conversation that's taking place here on the faith traditions in the way they are traditionally understood. And I just want some insight on this about the apostolic succession for bishops and the schism between the Western and Eastern branches of the Church.

Teal: Well, I think of the Church in the West in terms of Roman Catholic and Protestant traditions and the Church in the East in terms of the Orthodox. I do recognize apostolic succession, but there are many complex and nuanced schisms over this issue. Now, two weeks ago, the patriarchate of Moscow and the patriarchate of Constantinople divided. This doesn't mean they don't think there are proper ministers with apostolic succession, but there is a whole question about what apostolic succession means. Does it mean that there has to be a tangible, physical passing on of that apostolic authority by the laying on of hands? Is it sort of like a drainpipe where you've got to have everything connected? Or is it more like something from the Protestant wing of the reformed Church of England, which wasn't really concerned about apostolic succession because it was much more about the Bible, and there was yet another argument that there was a residual apostolic succession. One of the things that happened after the Oxford Movement was a papal investigation that took place to see whether or not Anglican priests could claim to have apostolic succession (like the Old Catholics), and in wonderful clarity, perhaps less charity, they said Anglican orders were "absolutely null and utterly void", in other words, completely powerless.[9] So that, in a sense, is where the Anglican Church stands in the definition of the Catholic Church: the Anglican ministers are ministers, but they're not priests. And one of the things that you talked about was apostolic succession and restoring the priesthood. Temple rather than church—is that the reason why you build temples in Chorley, and indeed all over the world?

Holland: Thank you for raising that, Andrew, because people often have that very question. We have our regular worship, our regular daily, weekly worship, in chapels and meeting houses as almost any church would do. The temple is distinct with us in the sense that it is reserved for the highest ordinances, the most sacred sacraments, and not for the weekly worship where we gather as families, sing our hymns, and have our prayers. For example, the work that we talked about for the deceased, where we do work for our own kindred dead, our own ancestors, is reserved for a temple. The temple is not a secret. In fact, any time we build or renovate a temple, we have an open house so people can come in and see its beauty. Once it's dedicated, however, it takes on a special sanctity, and it is reserved for special, holy ordinances. We have 150-something temples (and counting), but we have probably twenty thousand chapels or meeting houses or other places of worship around the world for daily and weekly use. That is the distinction that we make for the two temples in the UK—London and Preston—you have mentioned.

Teal: And the priesthood for all the believers, in a sense, is apostolic succession, the Aaronic Priesthood. Is that how priesthood is construed?

Holland: Yes, we do make the priesthood available to all worthy males, but there is a worthiness aspect. One does not simply step forward and say, "I claim the priesthood" or "I have ordained myself". There is a process. We speak of keys; we talk about the transmission of keys by the laying on of hands, but the priesthood is universally available for the men who meet the worthiness standards. I hasten to stress that women and children all participate in the blessings of that priesthood as well. There is a male ordination involved, but the priesthood influences and affects all—men, women, and children. For example, babies can receive a priesthood blessing at birth. You and I were talking about this before this event and how it is the equivalent of your christening. So the priesthood is experienced by individuals and entire families from birth forward.

Question 4
I'm a philosopher, so I could talk about this all day. I love that excuse. Elder Holland started talking about the reasons members of The Church of Jesus Christ of Latter-day Saints are regarded as Christians; Christianity started with the doctrine of the Trinity, and then he went on to describe the oneness of the Godhead in a way. You could understand what he described in terms of being of one essence, of one nature but of three distinct personages. I heard you, Reverend Teal, express a willingness to rethink the way we describe the experience of God, the experience of divinity. So I guess my question is just how important do you think this physical oneness is? It seems to get

in the way so often of our chances to talk to each other, our treating each other with respect.

Holland: The wonder of today is all a tribute to Andrew Teal. You heard him introduce me and ask these questions. He knows more about what we believe and what we don't believe than some of our own members, and that is the proper way to have a gospel conversation. You knew that it was in Missouri that an extermination order was issued; you knew about the distinctiveness of the Book of Mormon; you are familiar with Joseph Smith's history. You knew that before I walked in this room. That is the way to cut through metaphysical difficulties. There might be some metaphysical challenges that arise along the way, but if they arise with common understanding and common vocabulary, then I think we can handle them courteously and comfortably. In short, we need to keep those first two great commandments, and that is the ultimate compliment to you today, Andrew. You have invited us with courtesy and knowing more about us than some of us know about ourselves. That truly is the ultimate compliment.

Teal: We need each other's eyes to see ourselves. I think this is why something living is going on.

Holland: And that's why we will find that good people have more in common than in difference. In regards to my own education regarding the Trinity, as a young man (like one of these young men back here with these missionary name tags on), I was quite sure that I knew everything that the apostolic Church believed, traditional Christianity believed, the Roman Catholic Church believed, and everybody else believed about the Trinity. Well, embarrassingly, I've learned that I didn't know very much about what they believed. But, if we can start talking about what we have in common, where we do agree, like we have in these kinds of conversations, then it is a lot easier to fine-tune the issues—we get more light and less heat. The differences may be significant, but if they are discussed in a spirit of goodwill, we can come to understanding. I get interviewed in many of the places I go. The only thing I have ever asked from a journalist or the one who is interviewing me is to please not tell me what I believe. So often someone will say, "Well, now you Mormons believe", and I have to stop them there and say, "Well, I am going to be interested in what you say because then I will tell you whether I believe that or not." It is just a lot nicer to do it the Andrew Teal way, who will say, "If I understand correctly, this is the Latter-day Saint position", or "Please tell us what you believe regarding . . . "; then the conversation starts at such an elevated level, at such a courteous and informed level. It often turns out we agree on more than we realize, and it gives us ground to discuss where we don't agree. I loved your word envisage; I loved your word hope. Could it possibly be that if we learn together in the spirit we have felt today, that we could be closer to true brotherhood and sisterhood than we thought possible? Closer together and not further apart? I really, truly believe that with all my heart.

Teal: Yes, me too. We've had a really marvellous time, and we have a wonderful note here to almost end on, but we wanted to leave it in case someone had a final question here.

Question 5

I guess I mostly just have a question about priesthood. And I was wondering what your understanding of priesthood is and why it requires a formal ordination. And obviously during different periods, the definition of priesthood has been known to many different groups of people, but that question is more of if the priesthood, or however God wants to interact with humanity, transcends this notion. Reverend Teal mentioned that it does, and Elder Holland mentioned how priesthood sort of affects all people: men, women, and children. So my question is basically what is the significance of ordination, and why do you need to control it in that formal sense?

Holland: Maybe that question is directed to me because we are the ones that say it requires ordination. I'm not sure what actually happens when hands are laid upon a person's head, but something is being communicated in that touch, that contact. And I do know that keys and authority must be held in order for one to give keys and authority to another. As for control and regulation, I've wondered if part of the answer is that ordination can be a protection against abuse and profligacy. Let me use a horrid, extreme example. Some evil, truly evil person might like to say, "Well, I claim the priesthood; I have it, and I'm God's spokesman, now I'll proceed to destroy that family, or ruin this nation, or hurt this individual, and will do it all in the name of the priesthood." That could still happen, I suppose, if an evil person somehow had hands laid on his head, but I think it is less likely if other worthy people are involved in the process. I think there is some governance, some actual protection against a "come one, come all" attitude of self-appointed priesthood. That's why I went to some length to make clear that worthiness distinction about the universal availability of the priesthood. We do believe in universal access, but we do not believe that one can just assume it, and I just wondered aloud with you, if that isn't some protection against one trying to claim a godly power in order to try to do some harm. At least there is a check and balance if one is found worthy by another who holds the keys to pronounce worthiness. God's house is a house of order, and the priesthood makes unique use of the word "order". It has the same root meaning as "ordain".

Teal: Thank you all for being here as we take these steps.

Holland: Thank you; I love you. I've just extended a formal invitation to Andrew to come to Brigham Young University next spring. We'll transport all of you over there for a continuation of this conversation. We promise to be just as courteous there as you were here. Please, I insist. What a generous and good man! Thank you, Andrew, thank you. I love you.

Notes

1. Lee M. McDonald, *The Formation of the Christian Biblical Canon*, rev. ed. (Peabody, MA: Hendrickson, 1995), pp. 255–56.
2. Quoted in C. Beaufort Moss, *The Divisions of Christendom: A Retrospect* (n.d.), p. 22.
3. Adaptation of original quote by Henry Martyn Field (1822–1907), long-time editor of *The Evangelist*.
4. Athanasius, for example, clearly has a vision of the necessity of apophatic theology to prevent our idolatry of language and intellectual constructs, as necessary as they are in the light of error. See his *Contra Arianos*.
5. Richard Hooker, *Laws* III.x.5.
6. Frederick William Faber, "There's a Wideness in God's Mercy", Hymnary.org, <https://hymnary.org/text/theres_a_wideness_in_gods_mercy>, accessed 14 August 2020.
7. Archimandrite Sophrony (Sakharov), Saint Silouan the Athonite (Maldon: Stavropegic Monastery of St. John the Baptist, 1991), p. 48; emphasis added.
8. "*O Felix Culpa*" (O Happy Fault), *Exsultet*.
9. Pope Leo XIII, Apostolicae Curae, <http://w2.vatican.va/content/leo-xiii/la/apost_letters/documents/litterae-apostolicae-apostolicae-curae-13-septembris-1896.html>, accessed 14 August 2020. Though often called a bull, it is actually listed as having the authority of an Apostolic Letter of 13 September 1896 and is quoted on the official Vatican website only in Latin: "pronunciamus et declaramus, ordinationes ritu anglicano actas, irritas prorsus fuisse et esse, omninoque nullas". ("We pronounce and declare that ordinations carried out according to the Anglican rite have been, and are, in every sense null and void.").

3

Christmas Comfort

Elder Jeffrey R. Holland

The following remarks were presented at the "Nine Lessons and Carols" service in the chapel of Pembroke College, University of Oxford on Sunday, 25 November 2018.

Below: Elder and Sister Holland singing with the choir

Approximately forty days after Mary's delivery of her child, she and Joseph took the baby, named Jesus, to the temple, where the infant was to be formally presented unto the Lord. As they made their way toward the temple, the Holy Spirit was resting upon a beloved, elderly man named Simeon. It was revealed to this gentle and venerable man that he would not die before seeing the Messiah, "the Lord's Messiah", as Luke phrases it (2:26). The Spirit then led him to the temple, where he saw a young carpenter and his wife enter the sanctuary with a newborn babe cradled in his mother's arms. Simeon, who had waited all his life for "the consolation of Israel", took that consolation in his arms, praised God, and said, "Master, now you are dismissing your servant in peace, according to your word; for my eyes have seen your salvation, . . . a light for revelation to the Gentiles and for glory to your people Israel" (Luke 2:25,29-30,32). Luke goes on to say, "And the child's father and mother were amazed at what was being said about him. Then Simeon blessed them and said to his mother Mary, 'This child is destined for the falling and the rising of many in Israel, and to be a sign that will be opposed so that the inner thoughts of many will be revealed - and a sword will pierce your own soul too" (Luke 2:33-35).

There's a profound Christmas message for me in the message this dear old man gave to beloved Mary in that first Christmas season. He was joyously happy, but his joy was not of the superficial kind. It was not without its testing and trying. In that sense, it didn't have much to do with toys, or trinkets, or tinsel, though these have their Christmas place. No, his joy had something to do with the fall and rising again of many in Israel, with the warning that this child's life, or more specifically his death, would be like a sword piercing through his beloved mother's soul. We might well ask, was such an ominous warning, such a fateful prophecy appropriate to this season of joy? Surely this was untimely, maybe even unseemly at that moment, when the Son of God was so young and tender and safe, and his mother so thrilled with his birth and his beauty. Well, I think our answer is, it was appropriate, and it was important. I submit that unless we see all the meaning and joy of Christmas the way old Simeon saw it all (and, in a sense, forced Joseph and Mary to see it)—the whole of Christ's life, the profound mission, the end as well as the beginning—then Christmas will be just another day off work with food and fun and football, and a measure of personal loneliness and family sorrow for some. The true meaning, the unique, joyous meaning of the birth of this baby was not confined to those first hours in Bethlehem but would be realized in the life he would lead and in his death, in his triumphant atoning sacrifice (remember why Joseph and Mary were in the temple) and in his prison-bursting Resurrection. These are the realities that make Christmas joyful.

But to be true to the complete experience, we must, on occasion, speak of Christmases and other days in our individual and collective lives that for whatever reason may not be as joyful or do not seem to be the season to be jolly. May I indulge in a personal reminiscence in this regard?

On the evening of 23 December 1976, my father underwent surgery to relieve the effect of osteoarthritis in the vertebrae of his back. The surgery was successful, but near the conclusion of it he suffered a major heart attack. Eight hours later in recovery he suffered another one. From those two attacks, he sustained massive damage to a heart that was already defective from an illness suffered in his youth. By the time we finally got to see him, wired and tubed, grey and unconscious, it was mid afternoon on 24 December, Christmas Eve. "Magnificent timing," I muttered to no one in particular. The day drew to an end without much change. The lights of Christmas Eve came on and then turned off. It was dark and lonely. I sat and paced and prayed alone in a hospital unfamiliar to me. I was feeling pretty sorry for myself. "Why does it have to be like this?" I thought. "Why does this have to be on Christmas? Of all the times to lose your dad, did it have to be on Christmas?" I confess that I was muttering things aloud by then as I walked what surely must have been every inch of the public space and a fair share of the private space in that hospital.

Then, at 3:00 a.m. or so, early in the morning in a very quiet hospital, immersed as I was in some sorrow and a lot of self-pity, heaven sent me a small, personal, pre-packaged revelation: a tiny Christmas declaration. In the midst of my mumbling about the very poor calendaring of all this, I heard the clear, unbroken cry of a baby. It truly startled me. Only then did I realize that I, in my wandering, had gone near the maternity ward, somewhere, I suppose, near the nursery. To this day, I do not know just where that baby was or how I heard it, but I like to think it was a brand-new baby, taking perhaps that first breath and announcing that he or she had arrived in the world, a fact of which everyone was supposed to take note. In that moment, it was as if the Lord had sent me a theological wake-up call: "Listen, Jeffrey. This is the happiest night in the whole year for some young couple who may otherwise be poor as church mice. Perhaps this is their first baby; perhaps he or she is their own personal consolation of Israel; perhaps he or she is the only consolation they have right now in what otherwise may be a difficult life. In any case, they already love this baby and this baby already loves them." And think of the calendaring: born on Christmas Day! What a reminder of God's grace and timing. Whatever pain may lie ahead, whatever sword may pierce their souls from time to time in life, they will be triumphant because of another birth, because the Prince of Peace was also born that same day, "once in royal David's city".[1]

Furthermore, it dawned on me that those could have been my own young parents, who were also impoverished when I was born. I was a December baby, and my mother never wearied of telling me that that was her happiest Christmas ever. Birth, and life, and death, and salvation—the whole divine experience in all its richness and complexity—these are God's Christmas gifts to us, all of them, and we receive them as a package—a Christmas package.

I learned something about eternal life that Christmas as well as something about the life of Jesus of Nazareth. With new eyes then, that morning, I went back to look in on my father, the great gift giver who was starting to make his way out of the world on Christmas Day.[2] He was doing so on the wings of the greatest gift ever given: the Atonement and Resurrection of the Lord Jesus Christ. I thought of another father who gave that gift, "For God so loved the world, that he gave his only Son, so that everyone who believes in him may not perish but may have eternal life" (John 3:16). Yes, perhaps the most important visitor of all in that first Christmas season may have been old Simeon, who, not in the absence of hard days and long years and swords that pierce hearts, but because of them would sing with us tonight of the Babe of Bethlehem's birth and life and victory over death. "Joy to the world", Simeon would sing, "the Lord is come; let earth receive her King! . . . Rejoice! Rejoice when Jesus reigns, and Saints their songs employ. No more will sin and sorrow grow, nor thorns infest the ground; He'll come and make the blessings flow far as the curse was found. Rejoice, rejoice in the Most High, . . . and ever worship God."³

I so rejoice, and I so worship with you in this blessed season of the year, in the name of Jesus Christ, Amen.

Notes

1. Cecil Frances Alexander, "Once in Royal David's City", *Hymns* (Salt Lake City: The Church of Jesus Christ of Latter-day Saints, 1985), no. 205.
2. My father never regained strength and died near the start of the new year.
3. Isaac Watts, "Joy to the World", *Hymns*, no. 201.

Below: The Revd Dr Andrew Teal singing with the choir

EU GPSR Authorized Representative:

LOGOS EUROPE, 9 rue Nicolas Poussin, 17000 La Rochelle, France

contact@logoseurope.eu

www.ingramcontent.com/pod-product-compliance
Lightning Source LLC
Chambersburg PA
CBHW071626170426
43195CB00038B/2138